TOY DOGS

THE BREEDS AND STANDARDS
AS RECOGNIZED BY

THE AMERICAN KENNEL CLUB

WITH AN INTRODUCTION BY
CHARLES T. INGLEE
Executive Vice President

Majority of photographs by R. W. Tauskey

NEW YORK
G. HOWARD WATT, INC.
1935

Copyright, 1935, by
G. HOWARD WATT, INC.

All rights reserved

PRINTED IN THE UNITED STATES OF AMERICA

PREFACE

This book is offered to the public by The American Kennel Club in response to the many requests received by it from dog owners throughout the United States who felt there existed a need for an official publication giving the latest standards and also the origin and histories of the different recognized breeds of dogs in this country.

In the main each standard and historical article as presented, is the one drawn up by the breed club of this country or, if none existed here, the country where the breed originated or is now most popular. The American Kennel Club, beyond endeavoring to present the latest official standard of each breed, assumes no responsibility for the drawing up or forming of these standards and articles.

It was felt that each breed should be represented or pictured by illustration. Sketches of the ideal dog of each breed were suggested. After a careful deliberation of the subject, it was decided this would be unwise as it would mean presenting only the artist's conception of the ideal type, which might very possibly not conform with that of the majority interested in that particular breed. Therefore, illustrations of actual photographs of dogs considered to be typical specimens of their breeds, are used. In order to obtain these, requests were made to the different breed clubs for a photograph of a dog considered to be a typical specimen. The majority of the photographs, so submitted, appear in the book. In some

PREFACE

instances, however, the club was unable to furnish a photograph suitable for reproduction, in which case a more typical picture was selected. It however is understood that these photographs are not published as being examples of perfect dogs but only prints them as being pictures of the most typical type procurable of each breed.

For help in the preparation of this book, The American Kennel Club desires to extend its most grateful thanks to the secretaries and other officers of the various breed clubs, both in this country and abroad, and to all who have so kindly assisted in the effort and thus made the work easier of accomplishment and more valuable in result.

CONTENTS

	PAGE
Preface	v
Note	viii
Introduction	ix

Group V
TOY DOGS
The Breeds and Illustrations

Chihuahuas	3
English Toy Spaniels	9
Griffons (Brussels)	15
Italian Greyhounds	21
Japanese Spaniels	25
Maltese	31
Mexican Hairless	37
Papillons	41
Pekingese	47
Pinschers (Miniature)	53
Pomeranians	59
Pugs	65
Toy Manchester Terriers	69
Toy Poodle	73
Yorkshire Terriers	79
Glossary of Technical Terms Relating to Dogs	87

NOTE

Various States throughout the United States of America have laws which forbid the cropping or cutting of dog's ears, or the possession of dogs whose ears have been cropped in those States subsequent to the enactment of such laws

INTRODUCTION

In modern times there has come a fuller appreciation of the dog and his importance to man; yet the bond of companionship that links man and dog extends back to the dim beginnings of civilization. In the history of the dog lies the history of all peoples; in the development of the dog is the development of all races; and in the love of the dog is reflected the finer instincts of all human kind.

Man and dog have grown apace through the generations. Theirs is a partnership that has endured through happiness and sorrow; has persisted when cataclysmic disaster shook the earth; and has been of such force as to catch the attention of our greatest philosophers.

If there is any single service that can aid the cause of the dog and his many pure-bred varieties it is the collecing of the countless fragments of his history from the literature of the world. And this is the work that finds fruition in the publishing by the American Kennel Club of the six books comprising the group edition of PURE BRED DOGS. These books are submitted to dog lovers with the conviction that they are the most complete and authentic works ever published on the recognized breeds of the world. They show facts in dozens of cases where only hazy speculation has been true in the past. The men and women who have contributed to these pages —penning the histories of more breeds than are recognized by any other nation in the world—have left few ancient or modern sources unplumbed to gather material for their articles which have been edited with a constantly challenging, critical eye that demanded authentic foundation for every statement. In some instances the Breed Associations or breed representatives of various breeds did not supply the historical information required and acknowledgment is hereby given to Mr. Arthur Frederick

INTRODUCTION

Jones for his invaluable assistance in writing and tracing the origins.

The dog is mentioned in some of the earliest parts of the Old Testament and in the course of some forty references to him in the Bible one learns that there was great differentiation in breeds and types, and of all the basic lore on the dog, the most definite has been bequeathed to us by the ancient Egyptians and Assyrians. The earliest picture showing dogs is found on the Tomb of Amten, in Egypt, which dates to the 4th Dynasty, or between 3500 and 4000 B.C. Hunting scenes are depicted showing dogs of the sight-hound type. And from later Egyptian Dynasties comes concrete evidence of three other types of dog. Monuments in Assyria before the Christian Era give us more views of the old kinds of dogs.

Like man and with man, the dog has migrated ever Westward. He has made his home wherever and however his master has been satisfied; seeking only that small measure of affection from man which is so slight when set beside what the dog has to return. And, in this second third of the twentieth century, the dog finds his greatest home in the United States of America; in a country that now recognizes more pure breeds than any other in the world.

Every year brings a broadening of the horizon of knowledge in all fields, and it is possible that in time to come we will know much more than we do today about dogs. But, until that time arrives, it is my firm belief that this latest group edition of PURE BRED DOGS should serve as the most authoritative text-books of the dog lover.

TOY DOGS

CHIHUAHUA

CHIHUAHUAS

While little or nothing is known of the previous history of the Toltecs, it has been adequately established that they existed in what is now Mexico as early as the ninth century A.D., and that during their several centuries of occupancy they had a breed of dog called the Techichi. This dog was small, but not tiny, and was of a heavy-boned structure. His coat was long. Still, his most distinctive feature was his muteness.

The Techichi, regarded as indigenous to Central America, is the progenitor of the Chihuahua that now enjoys popularity throughout the United States where he has been bred to his greatest perfection. No records of the Techichi are, so far, available prior to the ninth century, but it seems quite probable that its ancestors were in the locality prior to the advent of the Maya tribes about the fifth century.

The evidence that firmly establishes the Techichi to the Toltec period is found in pictures carved on stones. These stones may be found today in the Monastery of Huejotzingo, on the highway from Mexico City to Puebla. This monastery was constructed by the Franciscan Monks around 1530 from the materials of the existing Pyramids of Cholula, built by the Toltecs. The carvings give a full head view, and a picture of an entire dog that closely approximates the Chihuahua of modern times. There also are the remains of pyramid constructions, and likewise some pointers to the early existence of the Techichi at Chichen Itza in distant Yucatan.

TOYS

The Toltec civilization was centered principally around Tula, which is close to the present City of Mexico, and it is there that one finds the most abundant relics of this ancient breed. For that reason, there always has been some speculation regarding the discovery of the earliest specimens of the modern breed in the State of Chihuahua. The dogs were found, about 1850, in some old ruins close to Casas Grandes, said to be the remains of a palace built by Emperor Montezuma I.

The conclusions of K. de Blinde, a Mexican breeder and authority, who has spent years of personal investigation—traversing vast sections of the country on horseback—are that the present form of the Chihuahua evolved from the crossing of the Techichi and the small hairless dog brought from Asia, over the land bridge where now runs the Bering Strait to Alaska. This hairless dog, similar to the one found today in China, was responsible for the reduction in size.

The Aztec conquerors of the Toltecs flourished for several centuries, and just prior to the coming of Hernan Cortes the civilization was at a very high state and the wealth was prodigious. The dogs of the rich were highly regarded, and the blue colored ones were held as sacred. Paradoxical as it seems, the common people found little use for this same breed, and there are even tales that they were eaten.

The storm-like career of Cortes in Mexico during 1519–20 left little of either Aztec wealth or civilization. Practically all Montezuma's possessions were wrung from his dying hands, and it is only natural that his dogs became lost for several centuries.

While the Techichi had its principal home in Mexico there is an historic letter written by Christopher Columbus to the King of Spain that adds a curious note to the knowledge of the breed. Reporting on the seizure of the present island of Cuba, Columbus stated that he found; "A small kind of dogs, which were mute and did not bark, as usual, but were domesticated." These dogs could not have been taken to Cuba by the Aztecs, who were not a seafaring people.

Legend and history are rich in tales of the ancestors of the present Chihuahua. He is described as a popular pet, as well as a religious necessity, among the ancient Toltec tribes and later among the Aztecs. Archeologists have discovered remains of this breed in human graves in Mexico and in parts of the United States.

This phenomenon is believed due to the part the dog played in the religious and mythological life of the Aztecs. He was employed in connection with the worship of Deities; with the voyage of the soul in the underworld; and in relation to the human body. The sacrifice of a dog with a red skin, burning it to ashes with the corpse of the deceased, the sins of the human were supposed to be transferred to the dog, and the indignation of the deity thus averted. The dog also was credited with guiding the human soul through the dark and terrible regions of the underworld, fighting off the evil spirits and leading the soul of the deceased safely to its ultimate destination.

The modern Chihuahua is quite different from his early ancestors, and is regarded by its fanciers as one of the most alert and intelligent dogs in existence. Its variegated colors are an attractive feature, the breed ranging from snow white to jet black. Mexico favors the jet black with tan markings, and the black and white spotted. The United States prefers the solid colors.

American breeders have produced a diminutive type that has few comparisons, even among other breeds, for

TOYS

smallness, symmetry and perfection of conformation, as well as for its intelligence and alertness. Incidentally, it is a curious aspect of the Chihuahua's intelligence that it is clannish, recognizing and preferring its own kind, and, as a rule, not liking other breeds. The smooth-coated are the most numerous in the United States, and the most clannish, but the long-coated Chihuahua is rapidly increasing. It has all the characteristics of the smooth.

DESCRIPTION AND STANDARD OF POINTS
(Adopted by The Chihuahua Club of America and Approved by The American Kennel Club, August 14, 1934)

Head.—Well rounded "apple dome" skull, with molera. Cheeks and jaws lean. Nose moderately short, slightly pointed, self-colored, pink or black, depending on the color of the dog. (e.g., in moles, blues, chocolates, the noses are self-colored; in blond types, pink.)

Ears.—Large, held erect, flaring to sides at about an angle of 45 degrees and less.

Teeth.—Level.

Eyes.—Full, but not protruding, balanced, set well apart, dark, ruby, luminous.

Neck.—Slightly arched, gracefully sloping into lean shoulders, ruff or close haired about the neck. Shoulders lean, sloping into a slightly broadening support above straight forelegs that are set well under, giving free play at the elbows, with fine pasterns. Shoulders should be well up, giving balance and soundness, sloping into a level back, and never "down" or low. This also gives a "chestiness" and strength of fore quarters, yet none of the "bulldog" chest, but plenty of brisket.

Back.—Level, slightly longer than the height. (Short back desired in males.)

Feet.—Small, toes well split up, but not spread, pads cushioned.

CHIHUAHUAS

Is neither the "hare" nor the "cat" foot. A dainty little foot, with nails moderately long.

Hind Quarters.—Muscular, hocks well apart, but not out, well let down, firm sturdy action.

Tail.—Moderately long, (when not a natural bob, or tail-less). Carried cycle, either up or out, but not tucked under. Hair on the tail in harmony with the coat of the body, preferred furry. Bob-tails and tail-less, so-born, are not against a good dog.

Coat.—In the "smooths" should be of a soft, smooth texture, close and glossy. In dark colors, well placed over the body and neck, more scanty on the head and ears. The long-haired should have fringed ears, legs and tail with the coat on the body semi-long, soft and silken, similar to the coat of the Papillon.

Color.—Any; solid or marked or splashed.

Weight.—One to six pounds. Two to four pounds preferable. If two dogs are equally good the more diminutive is preferred.

General Appearance.—A graceful, alert, swift-moving little dog with saucy expression, compact, with terrier qualities.

Disqualification.—Cropped tail, broken down or cropped ears.

SCALE OF POINTS

	Points
Head	20
Body	20
Coat	10
Tail	5
Color	5
Legs	10
Weight	10
General appearance and action	20
Total	100

ENGLISH TOY SPANIEL

ENGLISH TOY SPANIELS

Since the whole spread of civilization has been from the East to the West, it is only natural that most of our oldest breeds of dog should trace their origin to the eastern countries. Such is the case of the English Toy Spaniels, those affectionate, intelligent, little dogs that captivated royalty, the aristocrats, and the wealthy for at least three centuries.

It has been a widespread fallacy that the Toy Spaniels made their first appearance in England during the reign of King Charles II, in the seventeenth century, for it was in honor of this sovereign that the black and tan variety took its name. Yet the Toy Spaniel had been known in England and in Scotland more than a hundred years before.

Just how long the Toy Spaniel had been known in Europe, particularly the south of Europe, before it was carried to England, must remain a matter of doubt. Yet most authorities are agreed that it goes back to Japan, and possibly China of very ancient times.

According to Leighton, the English Toy Spaniel had its origin in Japan, from where it was taken to Spain, and from thence to England. Yet the extremely short nose of the breed might very easily be evidence that it went from Spain to Japan, where it developed its present characteristics. There is a story, also, that specimens of this toy breed were brought from Japan by Captain Saris, a British naval officer, in 1613. They were presents from the Emperor of Japan—every Japanese royal present always included dogs—to King James I.

TOYS

The tale of Captain Saris seems a logical one, but it cannot be accepted as marking the debut of the Toy Spaniel into England and Scotland. The breed was known in England long before that, for Dr. Johannes Caius, the celebrated professor and the physician to Queen Elizabeth, included it in his foundational work on "Englishe Dogges." He refers to it as the "Spaniell Gentle, otherwise called the Comforter." His other references stamp it as almost the identical dog of today.

While it is difficult to associate the Toy Spaniel with the austere Elizabeth; evidence that this breed was the favorite of the warmer-hearted Mary, Queen of Scots, in the same century, is much more acceptable. The early years of Mary, during the first third of the sixteenth century, were spent in France. When she returned to Scotland as Queen, she brought specimens of the breed with her, and these dogs remained her favorites up to the time of her execution. In fact, her especial pet refused to leave her, even on the scaffold.

All Toy Spaniels up to the time of King Charles II appear to have been of the black and tan variety, later called the King Charles. This king's favorites were brought over from France by Henrietta of Orleans, and one is described as a black and white.

The development of the other varieties, the Prince Charles, which is a tricolor of white, black and tan, the Ruby, which is chestnut red, and the Blenheim, which is white and chestnut red, occurred at later times. All are identical in their characteristics, with the exception of color. For a long time they were bred without any reference to color. Often the same litter would produce dogs of several varieties. It is only in modern times that the science of color breeding set the different varieties apart.

The history of the Blenheim variety seems rather more

ENGLISH TOY SPANIELS

definite than that of the King Charles, although in some ways incompatible with other data. The development of the Blenheim, or red and white, is credited to John Churchill, the first Duke of Marlborough. Churchill, famous soldier and diplomat, was made an Earl in 1689, and became a Duke in 1702. At that time he acquired Blenheim, which has been the family seat of the Marlboroughs ever since.

It is said by Ash that the first Duke received as a present from China a pair of red and white cocker spaniels, and that these dogs were the basis of his subsequent breeding. The Chinese origin of the breed is mentioned also by Lady de Gex, who claims that during the fifteenth and sixteenth centuries there were carried from China to Italy numerous specimens of both red and white, and black and white spaniels. These dogs subsequently were crossed with cockers and springers, intensifying the sporting instincts which the Toy still retains.

The Dukes of Marlborough bred the Blenheim variety for many generations, and apparently they did so without the infusion of much outside blood—unless it were that of the cocker and other varieties of spaniel. It was said by Scott, in 1800, that the Duke of Marlborough's Blenheims were the smallest and best cockers in England. They were used very successfully for woodcock shooting. And writers of a still later period describe the dogs found at Blenheim as larger than other specimens of the red and white. Also, the Marlborough strain did not have such exaggeratedly short noses.

Regardless of the early history of the English Toy Spaniels, it seems certain that many specimens of modern times trace their origin back to various small spaniels of England. Selective breeding has reduced them down

TOYS

to the limits of six to twelve pounds, but it has not altogether erased their natural hunting instincts.

DESCRIPTION AND STANDARD OF POINTS
(By Courtesy of The Toy Spaniel Club of America)

Note:—Under the ruling of the American Kennel Club, passed December 16, 1902, Prince Charles, King Charles, Ruby and Blenheim Spaniels will, after January 1, 1903, be classed together as English Toy Spaniels.

Head.—Should be well domed, and in good specimens is absolutely semi-globular, sometimes even extending beyond the half-circle, and absolutely projecting over the eyes, so as nearly to meet the upturned nose.

Eyes.—The eyes are set wide apart, with the eyelids square to the line of the face—not oblique or fox-like. The eyes themselves are large and dark as possible, so as to be generally considered black, their enormous pupils, which are absolutely of that color, increasing the description.

Stop.—The "stop," or hollow between the eyes, is well marked, as in the Bull-dog, or even more so; some good specimens exhibit a hollow deep enough to bury a small marble in it.

Nose.—The nose must be short and well turned up between the eyes, and without any indication of artificial displacement afforded by a deviation to either side. The color of the end should be black, and it should be both deep and wide with open nostrils. A light colored nose is objectionable, but shall not disqualify.

Jaw.—The muzzle must be square and deep, and the lower jaw wide between the branches, leaving plenty of space for the tongue, and for the attachment of the lower lips, which should completely conceal the teeth. It should also be turned up or "finished," so as to allow of its meeting the end of the upper jaw, turned up in a similar way as above described. A protruding tongue is objectionable, but does not disqualify.

Ears.—The ears must be long, so as to approach the ground. In an average-sized dog they measure 20 inches from tip to tip, and some reach 22 inches or even a trifle more. They should be set low

ENGLISH TOY SPANIELS

down on the head and hang flat to the sides of the cheeks, and be heavy feathered.

Size.—The most desirable size is from 9 pounds to 12 pounds.

Shape.—In compactness of shape these Spaniels almost rival the Pug, but the length of coat adds greatly to the apparent bulk, as the body, when the coat is wetted, looks small in comparison with that dog. Still, it ought to be decidedly "cobby," with strong stout legs, short broad back and wide chest.

Coat.—The coat should be long, silky, soft and wavy, but not curly. There should be a profuse mane, extending well down in the front of the chest. The feather should be well displayed on the ears and feet, and in the latter case so thickly as to give the appearance of being webbed. It is also carried well up the backs of the legs. In the Black and Tan the feather on the ears is very long and profuse, exceeding that of the Blenheim by an inch or more. The feather on the tail (which is cut to the length of about $1\frac{1}{2}$ inches) should be silky, and from 3 to 4 inches in length, constituting a marked "flag" of a square shape, and not carried above the level of the back.

Color.—The color varies with the variety. The black and tan is a rich glossy black and deep mahogany tan; tan spots over the eyes, and the usual markings on the muzzle, chest and legs are also required. The ruby is a rich chestnut red, and is whole-colored. The presence of a few white hairs *intermixed with the black* on the chest of a Black and Tan, or *intermixed with the red* on the chest of a Ruby Spaniel, shall carry *weight against* a dog, but shall not in itself absolutely disqualify; but a white patch on the chest or white on any other part of a Black and Tan or Ruby Spaniel shall be a disqualification. The Blenheim must on no account be whole-colored, but should have a ground of pure pearly white, with bright rich chestnut or ruby red markings evenly distributed in large patches.

The ears and cheeks should be red, with a blaze of white extending from the nose up the forehead, and ending between the ears in a crescentic curve. In the center of this blaze at the top of the forehead there should be a clear "spot" of red, of the size of a sixpence. The tri-color should in part have the tan of the Black and Tan, with markings like the Blenheim in black instead of red on a pearly-white ground. The ears and under the tail should also be

TOYS

lined with tan. The tri-color has no "spot," that beauty being peculiarly the property of the Blenheim.

Scale of Points

King Charles, or Black and Tan. Prince Charles, White, with Black and Tan Markings. Ruby, or Red

	Points
Symmetry, condition, size and soundness of limb	20
Head	15
Stop	5
Muzzle	10
Eyes	10
Ears	15
Coat and feathering	15
Color	10
Total	100

Blenheim or White with Red Markings

	Points
Symmetry, condition, size and soundness of limb	15
Head	15
Stop	5
Muzzle	10
Eyes	10
Ears	10
Coat and feathering	15
Color and markings	15
Spot	5
Total	100

The above standard was adopted at the General Meeting of the Toy Spaniel Club of America held October 19, 1909.

GRIFFON (*Brussels*)

GRIFFONS (BRUSSELS)

(By Courtesy of Brussels Griffon Club of America)

The Brussels Griffon is not a dog of beauty as measured by the accepted standards but one teeming with personality, and for that reason it is not surprising that he makes lasting friends wherever he is known. He comes of neither an exalted nor an ancient lineage, yet is one of the most distinctive and unusual of all dogs. "Magnum in parvo" describes him most aptly. Although classified as a Toy Dog, there is nothing of the pampered pet in the typical Brussels Griffon, a bundle of jaunty good nature whose keynote is insouisance from his very turned up nose to the tip of his gaily carried tail. No matter what change of fortune the years may bring, he promises to remain the delightful little Belgian street urchin to the end of time.

His ancestry is interesting in that the German Affenpinscher as well as the Belgian street dog (which combined, were the true foundation from which our Griffons emanated) are both practically extinct and there is only the most meagre data available on both of these seventeenth century (or older) breeds. To all accounts, in Belgium there was a strong conformity to a distinct type in the peasants' dogs of that epoch. These dogs were nearly as large as our fox terriers but thickly built, as are most Belgian animals. Covered with a shaggy rough muddy colored coat and unlovely of feature, but intelligent and interesting of disposition, they were popularly termed "Griffons D'Ecurie," stable Griffons, and

TOYS

paid their keep by killing the stable vermin. They were loyal companions and it is not uncommon to run across mention of these dogs as "chiens barbus" in the old folk songs and tales of the period, for they were to be found in nearly every household.

On the other hand, the affenspinscher, from the few old photographs available, may be said to resemble the Yorkshire terrier in many particulars, the likeness being particularly noticeable in the head properties as well as in the length of both body and leg. Doubtless it was felt that the injection of affenspinscher blood into the then Griffons would serve to further increase the ratting ability of the Belgian dogs although since we lack definite proof, this last must remain a conjecture.

At some later date, the smooth coated Chinese Pug, already established in neighboring Holland, was used as a crossing with the Griffon. This cross breeding was responsible for the two types of coat which we have even in our present-day litters.

If there was any definite rhyme or reason for adding the Ruby Spaniel to this combination, we cannot say. Suffice that this breed was also brought into the picture and is largely responsible for the interesting facial characteristics and expression which are so much a part of our present-day dog but which have made impossible for him, the work to which he was once so well suited.

And so we come to the twentieth century Brussels Griffon, a small compact dog with a harsh reddish coat similar to that of the Irish Terrier, (or else a smooth coat traceable to the pug and termed Brabancon) with a short upturned face best described as a "speaking countenance" and a gay carriage.

The Griffon's super intelligence causes him to be sensitive and it is not at all uncommon for a young dog when

GRIFFONS (BRUSSELS)

in the presence of strangers, to display the same self-consciousness as does a child in its awkward teens. We must never lose sight of the fact that this is a breed which understands "English" and should always be treated accordingly. Although obedient and always easily managed, Griffons are sometimes difficult to break to the leash and this training should always be begun at a very early age. Strange as it may seem, it has been the experience of some of our leading exponents of the breed that the Brabancons display a marked stubbornness when it comes to going on a leash although in all other respects they are every bit as tractable as their rough brothers.

As a young puppy, he must be given the same intelligent care it is necessary to accord a puppy of any of the smaller breeds but the average sized Griffon becomes very sturdy as he matures and develops into a real comrade, being quite capable of holding his own on hikes and in swimming. The Griffon's ways are the more quaint and amusing because, when he acts he thinks! Therein lies the secret of his popularity.

DESCRIPTION AND STANDARD OF POINTS
(Adopted by Brussels Griffon Club of America, February 11, 1935, and Approved by The American Kennel Club, March 12, 1935)

General Appearance.—A toy dog, intelligent, alert, sturdy, with a thick-set short body, a smart carriage and set-up, attracting attention by an almost human expression.

Coat.—Reddish brown; a little black at the whiskers and chin is allowable. The coat should be wiry and dense. The harder and more wiry the texture of the coat is, the better. On no account should the dog look or feel woolly: and there should be no silky hair anywhere. The coat should not be too long so as to give

TOYS

the dog a shaggy appearance, but, at the same time it should show a marked and distinct difference all over from the smooth species.

Top Head.—Large and round, with a domed forehead and skull. It should be covered with a wiry rough coat slightly longer around the eyes, nose, cheeks and chin thus forming a fringe.

Ears.—Small and carried semi-erect; set rather high on the head.

Eyes.—Very large, black and well open. The eyelashes long and black. Eyelids edged with black. Eyes should be set well apart and prominent.

Nose.—Very black, excessively short; its tip being set back deeply between the eyes so as to form a lay-back. The nostrils large, the stop deep.

Lips.—Edged with black; not pendulous but well brought together giving a clean finish of mouth.

Chin.—Must be undershot, prominent and large with an upward sweep.

Jaws.—The incisors of the lower jaw should protrude over the upper incisors. The lower jaw should be rather broad.

Brisket.—Good size and deep.

Ribs.—Well sprung.

Back.—Level and short.

Tail.—Set and held high: cut to the one-third.

Forelegs.—Of medium length, set moderately wide apart and on a line with the point of the shoulders, straight in bone, and well muscled; pasterns short and strong.

Hindlegs.—Set true; bent at stifles; well let down; hocks turning neither in nor out; thighs strong and well muscled.

Feet.—Round, small and compact and turned neither in nor out, toes well arched. Black pads and toe nails preferred.

Weights.—For the class of dogs and bitches of a small size, the weight should not exceed 7 pounds. For the class of dogs and bitches of a large size, that is weighing more than 7 pounds, the weight should not exceed 11 pounds for dogs and 12 pounds for bitches.

Note:—In judging, quality should be of greater importance than weight, and general balance in any Griffon should take preced-

GRIFFONS (BRUSSELS)

ence over perfection of any single feature in an otherwise inferior specimen.

Minor Faults.—Light colored or small eyes; brown nails, teeth or tongue showing, light colored nose, toes joined on one or more feet.

Major Faults.—Silky topknot, both teeth and tongue showing simultaneously, wry mouth, button ears, a few white hairs on chest, unsoundness.

Disqualifications.—Dudley or butterfly nose; splashes of white on coat or chest; hanging tongue; the upper jaw overshot; looseness of stifle or any other major unsoundness. Dogs limping for no matter what reason, dogs completely blind or deaf, and dogs having undergone the operation of castration cannot be shown.

Scale of Points

Head

Head (forehead and skull)	5	
Nose and stop	10	
Eyes	5	
Chin and jaws	10	
Ears	5	35

Coat

Color	12	
Texture	13	25

Body and General Conformation

Body (brisket and rib)	15	
Legs	10	
Feet	5	
General appearance (tail carriage and topline)	10	40

GRIFFONS (Belgian)

The characteristics of the Belgian Griffon are the same as those of the Brussels Griffon with this difference—that the only colors

TOYS

admissible are: 1. Black and reddish brown mixed, with accompanying black mask and whiskers. 2. Black. 3. Black with reddish brown markings.

BRABANCONS.—The characteristics of the Brabancon are the same as those of the Brussels Griffon with this difference—that the Brabancon has a smooth short coat like that of the Boston Terrier or English Bulldog and the only colors admissible are: 1. Reddish brown. 2. Black with reddish brown markings.

Note:—The faults and disqualifications are the same in the Belgian Griffon and in the Brabancon as they are in the Brussels Griffon.

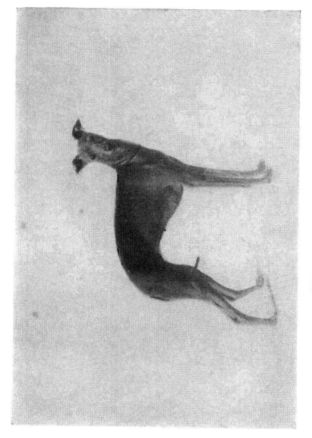

GREYHOUND (Italian)

ITALIAN GREYHOUNDS

Brought to England during the early years of the seventeenth century, in the reign of Charles I, the Italian Greyhound carried with it a glorious heritage as the favorite of royalty and the privileged classes. Never a dog of great use, it had won high esteem merely because of its marvelous disposition and its small size.

There is strong evidence that the Italian Greyhound was an effete favorite in the days of ancient Pompeii; and there are numerous relics throughout Italy that point to the breed as the only known pet dog for many centuries. The old Latin motto, "Cave Canem," or "beware of the dog," is found frequently in old Roman villas. According to Leighton, this did not refer to the huge mastiff, which invariably was kept chained, but to the tiny Italian Greyhound. The motto meant that guests should take care not to hurt the tiny pet of the matron, for he might easily be crushed by a careless step.

The date, and even the general period, at which the Italian Greyhound appeared as a distinct type is not recorded in any manuscript that has come down to us. It is known only that he has existed in his present form for more than 2,000 years. His origin, of course, is not difficult to deduce, for he carries no essential characteristics other than those of the large greyhound—characteristics that have been weakened and varied, but not radically changed. It is the general belief among the accepted authorities that the breed was dwarfed, intentionally, for pet purposes, from the gazehound of the ancients. Continual inbreeding finally led to a breed that produced some specimens as small as five pounds.

There is a possibility that the early development of the breed took place in Turkey, according to Dickie, but there remains very little supporting evidence for this conclusion. Later it became a favorite in Athens, and by the Middle Ages it was very popular throughout all of Southern Europe.

The type of the Italian Greyhound has not changed greatly from the earliest times down to the present, but like the majority of breeds it has undergone considerable refinement. The three centuries and more that the breed has been known in England and Scotland have brought it to a high state of perfection. The specimens owned by Mary Beatrice d'Easte of Modena, the Italian consort of James II, and those of Anne of Denmark, consort to James I, would not have done very well if taken into the ring against the delicate little greyhounds of Queen Victoria.

The Italian Greyhound, probably, reached its greatest heights during the Late-Victorian period. There were numerous big breeding kennels throughout England and Scotland, and it was then that the breed was introduced into the United States. It seems curious, indeed, that this breed so designed for the warm countries and so attuned to an even climate should have flourished so well under the dampness and the chilly atmospheres of England and Scotland. Still, the greatest breeder of modern times appears to have been W. Bruce of Falkirk, Scotland. When the breed came out to America it made its greatest early center in Pennsylvania, particularly at the kennels of Dr. F. H. Hoyt, who bred a succession of winners.

There are many interesting stories connected with the

ITALIAN GREYHOUNDS

Italian Greyhound. Perhaps the most curious of them all is that of King Lobengula, the black monarch of that perpetually warring South African people, the Matabele. One day while in Johannesburg, King Lobengula saw a specimen of the Italian Greyhound that was owned by Luscombe Searelle. The prancing manner of the dog so pleased the king that he made an offer for it. Mr. Searelle was reluctant to part with the dog, but finally succumbed to the pleas when the monarch promised him 200 head of cattle.

Another story is connected with Frederick the Great, King of Prussia. The king had a favorite Italian Greyhound that he carried with him wherever he went. And once, during the Seven Years' War, the tide of battle turned so quickly that Frederick found himself in a very precarious position. Dog in arms, he took refuge under the dry arch of a bridge. The dog clung to his royal master and did not utter a sound. Had the dog barked while the Austrian dragoons were passing, the fate of the king and of Prussia would have been decided right there. When this dog died, Frederick buried him with his own hands in the grounds of the palace in Berlin.

There have been certain yarns that attribute a sporting sense to the Italian Greyhound, but these all are discredited by those who have known the breed. It is solely a pet, and it has maintained that station throughout its long history.

DESCRIPTION AND STANDARD OF POINTS
(Courtesy of The Italian Greyhound Club, England)

General Appearance.—A miniature English Greyhound, more slender in all proportions, and of ideal elegance and grace in shape, symmetry and action.

TOYS

Head.—Skull, long, flat and narrow. Muzzle, very fine, nose dark, teeth level. Ears, rose shaped, placed well back, soft and delicate. Eyes, rather large, bright and full of expression.

Body.—Neck, long and gracefully arched. Shoulders, long and sloping. Chest, deep and narrow. Back, curved and drooping at the hind quarters.

Legs and Feet.—Forelegs, straight, set well under the shoulders, fine pasterns, small delicate bones. Hindlegs, hocks well let down, thighs muscular. Feet, the long "hare foot."

Tail.—Rather long, fine and with low carriage.

Coat.—Skin fine and supple, hair thin and glossy like satin.

Color.—All shades of fawn, red, mouse, blue, cream and white are recognized, black and tan terrier markings not allowed.

Action.—High stepping and free.

Size.—Two classes, one of eight pounds and under and one over eight pounds. A good small dog is preferable to an equally good large one but a good larger dog is preferable to a poor smaller one.

	Points
Skull	6
Muzzle	8
Ears	8
Eyes	5
Neck	8
Shoulders	5
Chest	5
Back	8
Forelegs	8
Hindlegs	8
Feet	8
Tail	8
Coat	4
Color	3
Action	8
Total	100

JAPANESE SPANIEL

JAPANESE SPANIELS

(By Courtesy of The Japanese Spaniel Club of America)

The Japanese Spaniel or Japanese Chin is known in every part of the world and is one of the oldest of all Toy Breeds.

The general belief is that they originally came from China many centuries ago, when an Emperor of China presented the Emperor of Japan with a pair of these dogs and that they developed as they are today, under the difference in climatic conditions. Most of the old Chinese temples have images of dogs, likewise do real old pottery and old embroideries, which under close observation resemble the Japanese Spaniel. These dogs were always kept among the people of noble birth, and once in awhile one was presented to a noted person, a diplomat, or to any foreigner who had rendered some great service to Japan.

Our Commodore Perry steamed into the Harbor of Wraga in 1853 and opened the country's trade to the world. He was presented with some of these dogs, and he in turn gave Queen Victoria of England a pair. Some of them in time came to America, but no record is obtainable of their final destination in America. Soon there was thieving among the Japanese Kennels and ships took them all over the world. They poured into this country about fifty years ago. Every incoming ship from the Orient had several, with equally as many buyers. Unfortunately they were not long lived, and when the World War broke and the supply was cut off we had to use what blood lines were left to improve and maintain our beloved breed. Japan too had her losses among her prized Chins, as earthquakes played havoc among the breeders. Since then a great many of the Japanese breeders have taken a fancy for other breeds and the supply has diminished there.

All over the world there are, however, Japanese Spaniels, there being breeders in England, France, Switzerland, Austria and Germany. These dogs breed so true to type that their high quality is still maintained.

The Japanese Spaniel is not a delicate dog. His Waterloo has been distemper, but this, we believe, has now been eradicated by inoculation. Since this has been his only enemy he should multiply rapidly in this country, from now on.

Most Japanese Spaniels are Black and White,—very black and very white,—however, there is a strain of white with lemon or red markings, including all shades from very pale lemon to the deepest red, and also including a brindle. Each must have nose color matching the markings, but always a dark eye, no matter what color the markings may be.

A Japanese Spaniel is a marvelous companion extremely bright and alert to its owner's wants. They are very game naturally, clean by nature and an ideal pet. They can thrive in any climate, can prosper in hot or cold quarters, but drafty quarters are dangerous.

The Jap is a sensitive creature, his feelings are readily hurt, and he has great likes and dislikes and never forgets friend or foe. Many times one may think his pet is not feeling just right, while in reality someone has hurt his feelings. These dogs are known to sulk in consequence of imaginary insults for days at a time. Treat

JAPANESE SPANIELS

them with consideration and kindness and no better pal is obtainable.

There are many types in these dogs, each correct.

1. First and foremost they must have Japanese character, must look like an Oriental, be aristocratic in appearance and stylish in action, and carriage. A larger dog loses in these qualifications, therefore only a small dog is considered of show type. However, he must not be weedy in makeup.
2. Certain types carry profuse coats, others shorter and coarser coats,—either is correct, but a woolly coat is not allowed. No two dogs are just alike, but a trained eye spots a good one.

We all have our goal, our preferences, but the one that is most sought after is the type with the head that has the short turned up nose, large well placed eyes, ears V-shaped and placed correctly at the top of the head. This type usually has very fine bone and nicely shaped body. In the same litter that contains this popular type of Japanese Spaniel there will, very likely also be found one with the straight nose which probably will also have a little length. His eyes, however, must be dark and set far apart and his "cushions" should be exaggerated. In this type dog there is usually found a fine but more of the bull type of body, which is desirable, and his ears to be correct must also be V-shaped. Either type must have the same aristocratic appearance and stylish action. Color may also be mixed in the same litter, if sire or dam has other than pure Black and White blood in its veins. Frequently a Lemon and White dog produces only Black and White offspring, and it may be several generations before the colors revert again. Years ago when a Black and White parent had too much Black on the body a Lemon and White dog was used to break the color. Again the Lemon and White frequently have more profusion of coat and this blood was often used to improve the class of hair. It is far more difficult to produce a perfect Lemon and White than a Black and White.

There is nothing prettier than a Japanese Spaniel pup when it commences to get its coat. They show their good points at an early age, and many believe the old adage, "as a Japanese Spaniel looks when he is exactly six weeks of age, so he finishes." He may go off before he is eighteen months old, but he should eventually look as good, or as bad, as he did on that eventful day when his weeks numbered six.

They do not as a rule have trouble in whelping, in spite of the fact that their heads are large, and they make good mothers. It is desirable to start feeding the youngsters after the third week, especially during the day, giving the mother the babies at night.

Anyone who at any time has had the good fortune to own a Japanese Spaniel will always be the owner of one, if possible, and surely will love them forever.

DESCRIPTION AND STANDARD OF POINTS
(Courtesy of The Japanese Spaniel Club of America)

General Appearance.—That of a lively, highbred little dog with dainty appearance, smart, compact carriage and profuse coat. These dogs should be essentially stylish in movement, lifting the feet high when in action, carrying the tail (which is heavily feathered, proudly curved or plumed) over the back. In size they vary considerably, but the smaller they are the better, provided type and quality are not sacrificed. When divided by weight, classes should be under and over seven pounds.

Head.—Should be large for the size of the dog, with broad skull, rounded in front.

JAPANESE SPANIELS

Eyes.—Large, dark, lustrous, rather prominent and set wide apart.

Ears.—Small and V-shaped, nicely feathered, set wide apart and high on the head and carried slightly forward.

Nose.—Very short in the muzzle part. The end or nose proper should be wide, with open nostrils, and must be the color of the dog's markings, i.e., black in black-marked dogs, and red or deep flesh color in red or lemon-marked dogs.

Neck.—Should be short and moderately thick.

Body.—Should be squarely and compactly built, wide in chest, "cobby" in shape. The length of the dog's body should be about its height.

Tail.—Must be well twisted to either right or left from root and carried up over back and flow on opposite side; it should be profusely covered with long hair (ring tails not desirable).

Legs.—The bones of the legs should be small, giving them a slender appearance, and they should be well feathered.

Feet.—Small and shaped somewhat long; the dog stands up on its toes somewhat. If feathered, the tufts should never increase the width of the foot, but only its length a trifle.

Coat.—Profuse, long, straight, rather silky. It should be absolutely free from wave or curl, and not lie too flat, but have a tendency to stand out, especially at the neck, so as to give a thick mane or ruff, which with profuse feathering on thighs and tail gives a very showy appearance.

Color.—The dogs should be either black and white or red and white, i.e., parti-colored. The term red includes all shades of sable, brindle, lemon and orange, but the brighter and clearer the red the better. The white should be clear white, and the color, whether black or red, should be evenly distributed, patches over the body, cheek and ears.

	Points
Head and neck	10
Eyes	10
Ears	5
Muzzle	10

TOYS

Nose	5
Body	15
Tail	10
Feet and legs	5
Coat and markings	15
Action	5
Size	10
Total	100

MALTESE

MALTESE

(By Courtesy of National Maltese Dog Club)

The Maltese dog is known as *Ye Ancient "Dogge of Malta."* For more than twenty-eight centuries "The Dogge of Malta" has been an aristocrat of the canine world.

Malta has been prominent in history from the earliest times. About 1500 B.C. it was settled by the Phoenicians, but from ancient ruins of the island, we know that other Mediterranean races lived there as far back as 3500 B.C. Many writers of antiquity have dwelt in glowing terms on the fame, opulence, and magnificence of Malta.

During the Roman domination, Diodorus, Cicero, and Valerius Maximus sang the praises of the Island.

It was celebrated over all the then known earth for its proficiency in the Arts and Crafts of peace and war, and for the high civilization of its inhabitants.

It was amid these surroundings and among these people that the tiny Maltese, the "Aristocrat of the Ancient World" was developed.

And among the Ancients, this lovely little animal was held in high esteem. The Greeks erected tombs to their Maltese dogs; and, in Greek ceramic art, from the fifth century onward, innumerable paintings of Maltese appear.

On a Greek vase, dating from about 500 B.C. a beautiful Maltese dog is shown—the vase was found at Vulci, and formed a part of the Bassegio collection.

TOYS

A very fine model of a Maltese dog was dug up in the Fayum, in Egypt. It is not unlikely that this was the kind of dog worshipped by the Egyptians.

At the time of the Apostle Paul, Publius, the Roman Governor of Malta, had a tiny Maltese named Issa—this he had painted in so life-like a manner that it was difficult to tell the picture from the live dog.

When the Apostle Paul, on his way to Rome (Acts 28), was shipwrecked on Malta, Publius was the Roman Governor of the Island. To commemorate the conversion of Publius, as well as the saving of Paul's life, the body of water called "St. Paul's Bay" was named after the Apostle.

Publius possessed a tiny Maltese named Issa of which he was very fond. The epigrammatic poet Martial (Marcus Valerius Martialis, born A.D. 38 at Bilbilis, in Spain), made this attachment famous in one of his celebrated epigrams which starts as follows:

"Issa is more frolicksome than Catulla's Sparrow. Issa is purer than a dove's kiss. Issa is gentler than a maiden. Issa is more precious than Indian Jems."

The epigram ended:

"Lest the last days that she sees light should snatch her from him forever, Publius has had the picture painted——"

Besides Martial, many other ancient authors discoursed on the beauty, the intelligence and the lovable qualities of Maltese dogs, including CALLIMACHUS THE ELDER (384-322 B.C.); STRABO (63 B.C.) PLINY THE ELDER (23-79 A.D.); SAINT CLEMENT of Alexandria, in the second century, A.D.; and others equally as celebrated.

Queens of old served out of golden vases the choicest of viands to their little Maltese.

The Ancients bred the Maltese very small.

MALTESE

Dr. Caius (1570 A.D.) physician to Queen Elizabeth who wrote in Latin says:

"There is among us another kind of highbred dogs, but outside the common run of these dogs (namely) those which CALLIMACHUS called Melitei from the Island of Melita. . . .

"That kind is *very small* indeed, and chiefly sought after for the pleasure and amusement of women. The smaller the kind, the more pleasing it is; so that they may carry them in their bosoms, in their beds, and in their arms while in their carriages."

Aldrovanus, who died in 1607, wrote of the early history of the breed in Latin. Aldrovanus says he saw one sold for the equivalent of $2,000. Considering the purchasing value of a dollar in the time of Queen Elizabeth, the price paid would be equal to a sum represented by five figures at this day.

Since the time of "Good Queen Bess," the Maltese has often been mentioned. The writers all drew attention to the *small size* of the dog. In 1607 E. Topsell wrote that they were not "bigger than common ferrets."

Almost 200 years later, LINNEAUS in 1792 referred to Maltese as "being about the size of Squirrels."

Danberton in his *History Naturelle* says that Maltese were so small "that ladies carried them in their sleeves."

The fact that Maltese have for many centuries been the household pets of people of culture, wealth and fastidious taste, very likely accounts for their great intelligence, refinement, fidelity and cleanliness.

They are Spaniels, not Terriers.

For more than twenty-eight centuries, history has consistently recorded that, although tiny, the Maltese was *healthy and spirited.* These *small dogs were bred,* and reproduced *small* dogs.

TOYS

To scientifically breed dogs, the "Eugenic Laws" must be followed.

A beautiful specimen of the Maltese in the arms of an old lady is painted by W. Powell Frith, R.A., in his celebrated picture of the "RAILWAY STATION."

DESCRIPTION AND STANDARD OF POINTS
(Courtesy of National Maltese Dog Club)

General Appearance.—Intelligent, sprightly, affectionate with long straight coat hanging evenly down each side, the parting extending from nose to root of tail. Although the frame is hidden beneath a mantle of hair, the general appearance should suggest a vigorous well proportioned body.

Weight.—Not to exceed seven pounds. Smaller the better. Under three pounds ideal.

Color.—Pure white.

Coat.—Long, straight, silky but strong and of even texture throughout. No undercoat.

Head.—In proportion to size of dog—should be of fair length: the *Skull* slightly round, rather broad between the ears and moderately well defined at the temples, i.e., exhibiting a moderate amount of stop and not in one straight line from nose to occiput bone.

Muzzle.—Not lean nor snipy but delicately proportioned.

Nose.—Black.

Ears.—Drop ears set slightly low, profusely covered with long hair.

Eyes.—Very dark—not too far apart—expression alert but gentle: black eye rims give a more beautiful expression.

Legs.—Short, straight, fine boned and well feathered.

Feet.—Small with long feathering.

Body and Shape.—Back short and level. Body low to ground, deep loins.

Tail and Carriage.—Tail well feathered with long hair, gracefully carried, its end resting on the hind quarters and side.

MALTESE

SCALE OF POSITIVE POINTS

Weight and size	20
Coat	20
Color	10
Body and shape	10
Tail and its carriage	10
Head	5
Eyes	5
Ears	5
Legs	5
Feet	5
Nose	5
Total	100

SCALE OF NEGATIVE POINTS

Hair clipped from face or feet	20
Kinky, curly or outstanding coat	15
Uneven texture of coat	10
Yellow or any color on ears or coat	10
Undershot or overshot jaws	10
Prominent or bulging eyes	10
Pig nose or deep stop	10
Roach back	5
Legginess	5
Butterfly or Dudley nose	5
Total	100

MEXICAN HAIRLESS

MEXICAN HAIRLESS

One of the most curious and distinctive breeds, the Mexican Hairless also is one of the oldest varieties of pure-bred dog in the world. Its hairlessness long has been one of the mysteries balking the most intensive investigation of scientists. The theory has been advanced that the lack of hair has been brought about by the temperature and the climate of the country in which the breed has existed. If this is true, the process of evolution must be extremely slow—for long-coated dogs have been known to exist under similar conditions for thousands of years.

Hairless dogs exist in many other parts of the world besides Mexico, and the theory which finds most acceptance—especially among Mexican authorities—is that this breed now found in relatively large quantities in the country below the Rio Grande is a descendant of the hairless dogs of China, where two somewhat similar breeds are known.

According to Sr. Blinde, the Mexican Hairless, or Biche, was established in Mexico when the Aztecs founded the Empire of Tenochtitlan in the Valley of Mexico. This tribe of Indian conquerors had brought the dog with them from Asia, crossing over the land bridge to Alaska at what is now the Bering Strait.

Just when the Aztecs migrated from Asia is a matter of some doubt, and there even is a supposition that the migration may have been in the opposite direction. However, the more reasonable one is that the Aztecs came from Asia. Had it been the other way, the hairless dog would have undoubtedly been discovered in other parts of North America, and it would not be found so often in different parts of Asia and Africa.

The Chinese Crested bears striking resemblance to the Mexican Hairless, and there is another hairless breed in China that is not so far removed from the Mexican variety. Then there is the Rampur dog of Southern India, likewise of the same general type. Another is the African sand dog, and somewhat similar dogs are found in Turkey, and in Japan. The South American dogs, of course, are regarded as closely related to the Mexican Hairless. The identical dog is found as far south as the Peruvian lowlands.

In Mexico the hairless dog is called commonly the "Biche," and this is another bond that links it to the old Indian civilization, for the word is an Aztec one meaning "naked."

Indications are that when the Biche started its travels with the Aztecs it was a much larger dog, believed to have been about the size of a small foxterrier. Yet it always was a light-boned animal, built on racy lines that might point to a very ancient descent from the greyhounds. Quite naturally the Aztecs could not take a great many dogs with them, and consequently the inbreeding brought a reduction in size.

The old legends that still persist, today, that the Mexican Hairless is possessed of healing qualities probably had their inception back in the Aztec days. In fact, this supplies a motive for an Indian people to have preserved this breed of dog through the generations. There is little or no reason to believe these stories, aside from the fact that heat often has a curative effect in certain instances, and the skin of this dog is hot to the touch. But from that simple basis grew many widespread beliefs, and in

MEXICAN HAIRLESS

time the ignorant were of the opinion that a person suffering from almost any disease would be cured of it if a dog of this breed were held close to the body. Specifically, one suffering from "rheumatism" could be relieved of it if the dog were placed at the feet.

The Mexican Hairless as recognized in the United States is a small, toy specimen, found in a variety of colors. Sometimes the skin is of a mottled nature, but that is less desirable. There is no hair on the body, but a slight fuzz on the top of the head, and sometimes a few hairs on the tail.

The great centers of the breed in Mexico are on the West Coast; Mazatlan, and Durango, but there also are relatively large numbers in the City of Mexico. Outside interest in the dog undoubtedly has proven a stimulus to breeders in Mexico, and the specimens of modern times are being bred to a high state of perfection.

DESCRIPTION AND STANDARD OF POINTS

The Mexican Hairless is a small, active dog, about the size of a small Fox Terrier, symmetrical and well proportioned, with rather broad chest and ribs and with slender legs.

Head.—Should be slender and skull narrow, cheeks lean, muzzle long and pointed. There should be a tuft of coarse hair on top of the skull, in the center but a bit forward, in some cases shadowing the brow.

Eyes.—Should not be too deep set but balanced and not bulging—eye rims pink or dark and the eyes themselves hazel, yellow or dark.

Neck.—Should be of good length, slender and well arched into flat shoulders and the chest rather broad, legs fairly long and slender, ribs well rounded and chest rather deep.

Back.—Should be level, rump slightly rounded.

Skin.—Smooth and soft, not wrinkled, any color, hot to touch, no hair whatever.

TOYS

Muscles and sinews well developed. A nervous tremor of muscles and sinews is characteristic like that of a nervous race horse.

Feet.—Should be hare feet, nails black in dark skin or pale in pale skin dogs.

Tail.—Long, smooth tail, carried out similar to that of Manchester Terrier. A little fuzz or hair on lower half of tail permitted.

Absence of tuft on top of the head is undesirable but not a disqualification.

Cut or broken ears or tail are disqualifications, likewise a fuzz or any hair, except as above described.

PAPILLON

PAPILLONS

(By Courtesy of The Papillon Club of America)

The Papillon is the modern development of those little dogs often seen pictured on rare old paintings or tapestries and known in the sixteenth century as "dwarf Spaniels." Rubens, Watteau, Fragonard and Boucher all depicted dogs of this breed upon their canvasses. For a time, the popularity of these dwarf Spaniels was so great, it was not surprising that many of the noble ladies of the day did not consider any of their portraits complete unless one of these elegant little dogs was also pictured with them. Madame de Pompadour was the proud possessor of two, Inez and Mimi by name. Marie Antoinette was another ardent fancier, while as early as 1545 there is record of one having been sold to a lady who later ascended to the throne of Poland.

It is Spain that we have to thank for the primary rise to fame of these little dogs, though Italy, with particular reference to the city of Bologna, probably developed the largest trade. Many were sold to the court of Louis XIV, who had his choice among those brought into France. The prices ran high and the chief trader, a Bolognese named Filipponi, developed a large business, not only with the court of France, but elsewhere. An interesting fact is that, lacking our modern means of transportation, most of the dogs were transferred from one country to the other upon the backs of mules.

As time went on, a change developed in the dwarf Spaniel which gave rise to the present-day appellation of "Papillon." During the days of Louis the Great, the dwarf Spaniel possessed large, drooping ears but gradually there came into being an erect-eared type, the ears being set obliquely upon the head and so fringed as to resemble closely the wings of a butterfly, from which the present breed derives its name. The causes of this change remain largely theoretical, but whatever they may be, we are now possessed of a toy dog whose type of body and coat is about the same as that of the original dwarf Spaniel of Spain and Italy but whose ears may be either erect or drooping. Both types may, and often do appear in the same litter. In continental Europe, as well as Great Britain, the drop-eared variety is called *Epagneul Nain,* although the breed as a whole carries the nomenclature of Papillon, as it does in this country. Here both types are as yet judged together and upon an equality.

Another change which has taken place in this breed concerns color. Originally, almost all were of solid color but today white predominates as a ground color, with patches or ticking of other colors.

The Papillon is one of the hardiest of dogs. It is unnecessary to coddle them in winter; they do not suffer particularly in severe hot weather; they do not contract disease easily; they delight in country activities and are equally contented in an apartment. As ratters, these little dogs make themselves extremely useful. Too small, for the most part, to kill a rat outright, they will worry it until it is completely weary and then dispatch it quickly. The bitches usually whelp easily and give little trouble in any way when rearing puppies.

The temperament and character of the Papillon invite the respect of all dog lovers. This breed is not only extremely affectionate and without snappy or irritable

PAPILLONS

tendencies, so as to commend it to women or children as a companion, but is so lively and courageous as to find itself becoming increasingly popular among boys and men.

Although this breed has been known and exhibited for many years in the United States by a privileged few, it was not until 1935 that Papillons were represented in the American Kennel Club by their own breed club, the Papillon Club of America.

DESCRIPTION AND STANDARD OF POINTS

(As Adopted by The Papillon Club of America, July, 1935, from the Standard of the Southern Counties Papillon Society, England. Approved by The American Kennel Club, August 13, 1935)

General Appearance.—A graceful little Toy Spaniel, slender and of lively and dainty action.

Varieties.—Two varieties are recognized. In one, the ears are carried upright at an oblique angle to the head, like the opened-out wings of a butterfly; in the other the ears are drop. The latter is known as Epagneul Nain.

Coat.—Short and smooth on the head, muzzle, forepart of front legs and on the back legs from the hocks downwards. Thin tufts of hair may be present between the toes and extend beyond them, but must not make the foot heavy; flat on the back and sides; abundant around neck, shoulders and breast; back part of front legs should be well-fringed, the length of fringes decreasing up to the wrist; breeches covered with long hair; tail covered with a very long, flowing plume.

Head.—Proportionate to the body and should appear small, being covered with short hair, while the remainder of the body is heavy-coated. The skull should be of medium width and slightly rounded between the ears. A fairly accentuated stop between skull and muzzle must not be too abrupt. The muzzle is abruptly thinner than the skull, getting more and more slender up to the nose;

not the wedge-shaped appearance of the Pomeranian. The muzzle should be moderately long; jaws well adjusted together. The lips must be tight and on no account pendant. The muzzle must not be flattened.

Eyes.—Rather large, round and set fairly low in the head. They should be dark in color. The expression must be lively and intelligent.

Ears.—The ears are set on at the sides in both the erect and drop, more backwards than forwards and fairly high. They must be sufficiently apart to show the slightly arched shape of the skull. In the erect variety the ears are carried obliquely like the spreading wings of a butterfly, the concha largely open and the inside entirely visible, crowned with silken hair. The ears should be large, the leather fine in texture but sufficiently strong to maintain the opened-up position while the dog is at attention or in action. The tip is rounded. In the drop variety the ears are similar except that they are carried drooping and flat against the head.

Neck.—Not short or thick, but lost in the coat.

Body.—Rather elongated; back fairly long and straight. Chest fairly deep; ribs slightly arched; stomach slightly turned up; loins moderately curving in.

Tail.—Set on fairly high and carried like a squirrel. The carriage of tail may be concealed with an abundant plume.

Shoulders.—Not too straight, very mobile and hidden by hair.

Fore Quarters.—Fine and straight, the back part covered with abundant fringes, diminishing to the wrist, the front covered with short hairs.

Thighs.—Fairly muscular, very mobile and well covered with hair.

Hind Quarters.—Slender, parallel and covered to the hocks with abundant breeches; hocks fairly high-placed and elbowed; the remainder covered with short and smooth hair.

Feet.—Thin, fairly elongated, toes close and arched, hair short, but fine tufts may appear between the toes and go beyond them provided they do not make the foot heavy.

Color.—Unicolor, of any color, provided the latter is pure, ex-

PAPILLONS

cept that the tawny shades may be smutty. Two-colored, white thrown into relief by patches and ticking; the size, shape and placement of the patches being without importance; a large saddle allowable. Tri-colored, similar to the two-colored except that the white is thrown into relief by spots, patches, or by both, of two colors. In both the two-colored and the tri-colored the skull should be divided by a white blaze. The body should be as white as possible.

PEKINGESE

PEKINGESE

(By Courtesy of The Pekingese Club of America)

Fascinating, not only by reason of its Oriental background but because of its distinctive personality and beauty as well, the Pekingese justly holds a commanding place in the world of the dog. That in ancient times the original Pekingese were held sacred in China, the land of their origin, is not to be disputed as many intricately carved Foo Dog idols of varying sizes and ranging in materials from ivory to bronze and jewel studded wood, have been handed down throughout the centuries. The exact date of the origin of the breed is a debatable point, the earliest known record of its existence being traceable to the Tang Dynasty of the eighth century. However, the very oldest strains (held only by the Imperial family) were kept pure, perhaps the more so because the theft of one of these sacred dogs was always punishable by a most horrible death. That the characteristics we seek to retain and perfect today were in evidence in the earliest Pekingese is shown by three of the names by which they were designated in ancient China. Some were called Lion Dogs, evidently because of their massive fronts, heavy manes and tapering hind quarters such as required by our present-day standards. We find a second group termed Sun Dogs because of their strikingly beautiful golden red coats. Since those early days, many other darker red shades have made their appearance and have become identified with certain strains but even today we see numerous Sun Dogs at our

TOYS

shows. A third appellation was that of Sleeve Dog, this being given only to those diminutive specimens which were carried about in the voluminous sleeves of the members of the Imperial household. Although there is no place for even the very tiniest Pekingese in the Occidental sleeve, the little ones have found a lasting place in the heart of the fancy and there are several clubs in existence functioning solely for the improvement of the under six pound Pekingese.

The introduction of the Pekingese into the western world occurred as a result of the looting of the Imperial Palace at Peking by the British in 1860. It is a matter of history that four Pekingese were found behind some draperies in the apartments of the Aunt of the Chinese Emperor. Apparently they were the particular pets of this lady, who committed suicide on the approach of the British troops. It is said that throughout the palace the bodies of many more of these dogs were found; the Chinese having killed them rather than have them fall into the hands of the Caucasians. The four Pekingese found by the English were of different colors and a fawn and white parti-color was the one presented to Queen Victoria on the return to Great Britain. Lord Hay and the Duke of Richmond kept the remainder and bred them.

Pekingese were not exhibited in England until 1893 when Mrs. Loftus Allen exhibited one at Chester. However, the undeniable beauty and interesting history of the breed placed it in the foreground where it has since remained.

The three dogs who were outstanding in the breed's earliest development in the Occident were Ah Cum and Mimosa, termed the "pillars of the Stud Book" in England, followed by a large black and tan specimen named

PEKINGESE

"Boxer," so called because he was obtained by Major Gwynne during the Boxer uprising in 1900. Curiously enough Boxer had a docked tail and so was never exhibited. He undoubtedly did more for the breed in the early part of the century than any other Pekingese.

That the Oriental dog took quick hold of the American fancy is evidenced by the age of the Pekingese Club of America which was formed nearly a quarter of a century ago and is not only one of the oldest but also one of the largest Specialty Clubs in the United States. So much for the introduction of the Pekingese to the Occident. The transplanting of the Pekingese into Western soil has in no way changed his personality. He combines marked dignity with an exasperating stubbornness which only serves to endear him the more to his owners. He is independent and regal in every gesture and it would be the greatest of indignities to attempt to make a "lap dog" out of him. Calm and good tempered, the Pekingese employs a condescendingly cordial attitude toward the world in general but in the privacy of his family circle enjoys nothing better than a good romp. Although never on the aggressive, he fears not even the devil himself and has never been known to turn tail and run. Incidentally he has plenty of stamina, much more in fact than have a number of the larger breeds, and is very easy to care for.

Since he has been made to come down from his pedestal in Chinese Temples the Pekingese has but one purpose in life, to give understanding companionship and loyalty to his owners. It may be truly said that the Pekingese fulfills his mission to perfection in every particular.

TOYS

DESCRIPTION AND STANDARD OF POINTS

(Adopted 1935 by The Pekingese Club of America and Approved by The American Kennel Club, May 14, 1935)

Expression.—Must suggest the Chinese origin of the Pekingese in its quaintness and individuality, resemblance to the lion in directness and independence and should imply courage, boldness, self-esteem and combativeness rather than prettiness, daintiness or delicacy.

Skull.—Massive, broad, wide and flat between the ears (not dome shaped), wide between the eyes.

Nose.—Black, broad, very short and flat.

Eyes.—Large, dark, prominent, round, lustrous.

Stop.—Deep.

Ears.—Heart shaped, not set too high, leather never long enough to come below the muzzle, nor carried erect, but rather drooping, long feather.

Muzzle.—Wrinkled, very short and broad, not overshot nor pointed. Strong, broad under jaw, teeth not to show.

Shape of Body.—Heavy in front, well sprung ribs, broad chest, falling away lighter behind, lion-like. Back level. Not too long in body; allowance made for longer body in bitch.

Legs.—Short forelegs, bones of forearm bowed, firm at shoulder; hindlegs lighter but firm and well shaped.

Feet.—Flat, toes turned out, not round, should stand well up on feet, not on ankles.

Action.—Fearless, free and strong, with slight roll.

Coat, Feather and Condition.—Long, with thick undercoat, straight and flat, not curly nor wavy, rather coarse, but soft; feather on thighs, legs, tail and toes long and profuse.

Mane.—Profuse, extending beyond the shoulder blades, forming ruff or frill round the neck.

Color.—All colors are allowable. Red, fawn, black, black and tan, sable, brindle, white and parti-color well defined: black masks and spectacles around the eyes, with lines to ears are desirable.

PEKINGESE

Definition of a Parti-Color Pekingese.—The coloring of a particolored dog must be broken on the body. No large portion of any one color should exist. White should be shown on the saddle. A dog of any solid color with white feet and chest is NOT a particolor.

Tail.—Set high; lying well over back to either side; long, profuse, straight feather.

Size.—Being a toy dog, medium size preferred, providing type and points are not sacrificed; extreme limit 14 pounds. Anything over must disqualify.

	Points
Expression	5
Skull	10
Nose	5
Eyes	5
Stop	5
Ears	5
Muzzle	5
Shape of body	15
Legs and feet	15
Coat, feather and condition	15
Tail	5
Action	10
Total	100

Penalizations.—Protruding tongue, badly blemished eye, overshot, wry mouth.

Disqualifications.—Blindness, docked tail, cropped ears, overweight, Dudley nose.

MINIATURE PINSCHER

PINSCHERS (MINIATURE)

(By Courtesy of The Miniature Pinscher Club of America, Inc.)

The Miniature Pinscher has been in existence for several centuries. Their native land is Germany, but they have been bred also in the Scandinavian Countries for a long time. The real development of the breed abroad started first in 1895 when the Pinscher Klub was formed in Germany. This Club is now called the Pinscher-Schnauzer Klub. It gave the breed its first standard.

From the time of the formation of the Pinscher Klub, the breed moved forward, both in type and popularity, but the real spurt began in 1905 and continued up to the World War. The war, of course, considerably handicapped forward progress in almost everything. After it, or beginning in 1919, the breeders and fanciers abroad again started the advancement of the Miniature Pinscher and through several importations to the United States breeding started here on a very limited and scattered scale.

There were, however, few Miniature Pinschers seen at dog shows in the United States before 1928 and the real start of the advancement of the breed began in 1929 when the Miniature Pinscher Club of America, Inc., was organized. The breed previously had been shown in the miscellaneous class in the dog shows. After the formation of the present Miniature Pinscher Club here and its acceptance as a member of the American Kennel Club,

TOYS

the breed became classified under the name of Miniature Pinscher, and a considerable upswing in breeding and showing became noticeable. The breed because of its small size has been put in the Toy Group. This little dog's popularity has steadily increased and as many as 34 entries of the breed often appear in dog shows. Many times there are just as many entries as of any other breed in the Toy Group.

Imported and American-bred dogs of this breed have won the Toy Group many times. One American-bred dog was awarded best in the Toy Group at the Chicago show of 1935.

Although the Miniature Pinscher is similar to a Doberman on a smaller scale, it has the nature and a way about itself suggesting a much larger dog. Therefore, it is noted as a watch dog and will bluff itself about, perhaps, in many cases better than a dog twice its size. It is a born show dog because of its attractive and smart appearance, and is noted for its active and lively temperament. Its gait is similar to that of a good hackney pony. The Miniature Pinscher is most intelligent and is often used on the stage because of its style, smartness and "pep."

For the above reasons and qualifications the breed has enjoyed the support of many socially prominent persons in Germany for a long time, and when the breed was finally introduced here a number of prominent people flocked to the fancy and to the support of it, many of them have become so attached to the Miniature Pinscher that they have established kennels of this, their favorite breed.

The owners of Miniature Pinschers will get great companionship from their pets. The close, slick coat requires

PINSCHERS (MINIATURE)

very little attention; they always look clean, and their fondness for home and master is exceptional.

If you like a small "Pinscher" with smart appearance and full of life, see them trotting around and "showing off," in some of the dog shows and you will have found what you are looking for.

DESCRIPTION AND STANDARD OF POINTS

(Adopted August, 1935, by The Miniature Pinscher Club of America, Inc., and Approved by The American Kennel Club)

General Appearance.—A miniature of the Doberman Pinscher, having on a modified scale most of its physical qualifications and specifications, viz., symmetrical proportions, sturdy though slim, pert, lively, attentive, with well distributed muscle formation and a carriage suggestive of an active and lively temperament.

General Faults.—Heavy set, coarse, poor quarters, too long or short coupled, knotty muscles, lethargic, timid or dull.

Head.—The head should be in correct proportion to the body. As viewed from the side—elongated and tapering, with only a slight drop to the muzzle, which should be parallel to the top of the skull. As viewed from the top—narrow with well fitted but not too prominent foreface. As viewed from the front—the skull appears flat, tapering forward to the muzzle. Muzzle itself strong rather than fine and delicate and in proportion to the head as a whole; cheeks and lips small, taut and closely adherent to each other. Teeth in perfect alignment and apposition.

Faults.—Too big or too small for body, too short or coarse, too long or fine or distorted, *top too broad,* foreface too prominent, skull too round or hollow with too much stop, poor teeth, *jaws undershot* or overshot.

Eyes.—Full, slightly oval, almost round, clear and bright, dark, even to a true black, set wide apart and fitted well into the sockets.

Faults.—Too round and full, too small or large, too bulging or deep-set, too close or far apart.

Ears.—Well set, and placed, firm, upstanding (or when legal, cropped short, pointed and upstanding).

TOYS

Faults.—Poorly set, placed low, weak or hanging, or poorly cropped.

Nose.—Black in black and tan, red or stag red.

Faults.—Brown or spotted in black and tan, red or stag red.

Neck.—Slightly arched, and gracefully curved, blending into the shoulders, relatively short, muscular, and free from throatiness. Length from occiput to withers equal distance from nose to occiput.

Faults.—Too straight or too curved. Too thick or too thin. Too long or short, knotty muscles, loose, flabby or wrinkled skin.

Body.—Compact, wedge shaped, muscular with well sprung ribs, the base line of which is level with the points of the elbows; well knit muscular quarters set wide apart, with back level or slightly sloping towards the rear. Length of males equals height, females may be slightly longer.

Faults.—Chest too narrow or barrel shaped, quarters too wide or too close to each other, too thin or too fat, sloping rump, swayback, roachback, wryback, hips higher or considerably lower than shoulders.

Legs and Feet.—Straight and upstanding as viewed from the front or rear with strong bone development and small joints; viewed from side—all adjacent bones should appear well angulated with well muscled stifles, short well developed hocks, well-knit flexible pasterns, strong, well-arched and closely knit toes with thick blunt nails.

Faults.—Bow or X-legs—too thick or too thin bone development, *large joints,* thin stifles, large or crooked hocks, floating knee caps, weak pasterns, spreading flat feet, feet turning in or out.

Tail.—Set high, broad, held erect and cropped 1 to 2 inches.

Faults.—Set too low, too thin, drooping, hanging or poorly cropped.

Coat.—Thick, hard, short, straight, and lustrous, closely adhering to and uniformly covering the body.

Faults.—Thin, too short, dull, upstanding, curly, dry, areas of various thickness *or bald spots.*

PINSCHERS (MINIATURE)

Color

1. Lustrous black with tan, rust-red or yellow markings on cheeks, lips, lower jaw, throat, above eyes, twin spots on chest, lower half of forelegs, inside of hindlegs and vent region. Black pencil stripes on toes. Faults—light colored or white, very dark or sooty spots,—in listed markings.
2. Solid yellow.
3. Solid red or stag-red.
4. Solid brown or brown with red or yellow markings.
5. Solid blue or blue toned with red or yellow markings.

Height.—Approximately eleven and a half inches at the shoulder or withers, with a slight variation permissible.

Faults.—Too small or too large.

Weight.—Five to ten pounds.

VALUE OF POINTS

	Points
General appearance and movement	25
Nose	5
Mouth	5
Eyes	5
Ears	5
Neck	5
Body	15
Feet	5
Color	10
Coat	15
Tail	5
Total number of points	100

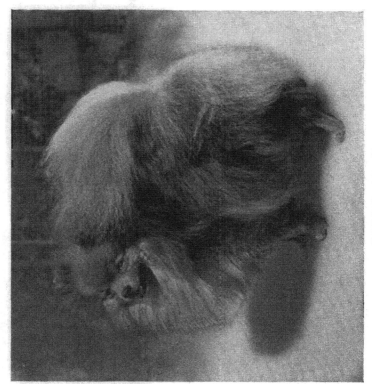

POMERANIAN

POMERANIANS

(By Courtesy of The American Pomeranian Club)

The Pomeranian, acclaimed by its admirers "the most alert and ever keen of all the Toy breeds" has shown marked improvement during the past decade both in type and size and profuseness of coat, the latter perhaps the paramount feature, that is, if one is guided by the standard where this feature is allowed twenty-five points with an added ten for color.

While it is true that a Pomeranian out of coat loses a deal of its charm, one must not overlook the important fact that coat, as one old-timer expressed it "is like charity, it oft-times covers many sins," hence his strong contention that "shape and make" with marked "Pom" character, that is, right on its toes, head erect with small well placed ears, expressing marked keenness, tail well over the back and carried flat to body, and merry action —so essential in a typical Pomeranian—are of much importance.

It is claimed by some that this fashionable breed with its essential characteristics has been traced back several centuries in different countries but there is no doubt in the mind of the majority that its place of origin was Pomerania—as the name seems to imply—and its forbears the large white Spitz bred down from the Iceland and Lapland sledge-dogs. Be it as it may, the breed was not well known until 1870 when the English Kennel Club recognized the then so-called "Spitzdog." Perhaps the nearest to the original type and size of the first

"Poms" exhibited in England was the somewhat large sable dog, Ruffle, shown by Mrs. Barrett and later brought to this country by Mrs. Smythe. Pomeranians were shown in the U. S. in the miscellaneous class as far back as 1892 but regular classification with winners class was not provided for them until 1900 at the New York show. In 1911 the American Pomeranian Club, already a member of the American Kennel Club, held its first specialty show of the breed, an event that has taken place annually ever since.

The majority of the early American winners were somewhat under six pounds in weight and had type and, generally speaking, good texture of coat but they lacked the profuseness of coat in evidence today and were somewhat heavier in bone and ears. However, present-day American-breds are marked improvements on the early winners; in fact, the patient efforts of the breeders have brought them nearer and nearer to the standard of perfection so that some American-breds have been able to go abroad and gain full quota of laurels as in the case of Ch. Pall Mall His Majesty which went to Europe and on several occasions beat all the Toy breeds for the coveted "Best in show." Over here home-bred Pomeranians have become constant and in many cases successful contenders for the highest honors at all-breed shows.

The diminutive size, docility of temper and vivacity of spirit plus sturdiness and stamina characteristic of the Poms make them adorable pets and great companions and their keen sense of hearing, boldness and alertness make them wonderful watch-dogs thus adding usefulness to beauty. In the show ring they make a most exquisite picture.

To visualize what constitutes real Pom type and character one has but to peruse the Club's standard which

POMERANIANS

follows and to commit to memory the accompanying photo of a very typical winner not forgetting that the general appearance of a typical Pom is that of a compact, short-coupled dog with marked activity, standing on tiny, cat-like feet, with profuse, stand-off coat, fox-like head with small, well carried ears and keen expression.

DESCRIPTION AND STANDARD OF POINTS
(By Courtesy of The American Pomeranian Club)

Appearance.—The Pomeranian in build and appearance should be a compact, short-coupled dog, well-knit in frame. His head and face should be foxlike, with small erect ears that appear sensible to every sound; he should exhibit great intelligence in his expression, docility in his disposition, and activity and buoyancy in his deportment.

Head.—The head should be somewhat foxy in outline, or wedge-shaped, the skull being slightly flat, large in proportion to the muzzle, which should finish rather fine, and be free from lippiness. The teeth should be level, and on no account undershot. The head in its profile may exhibit a little "stop," which, however, must not be too pronounced, and the hair on the head and face must be smooth or short-coated.

Eyes.—The eyes should be medium in size, rather oblique in shape, not set too wide apart, bright and dark in color, showing great intelligence and docility of temper. In a white dog, black rims around the eyes are preferable.

Ears.—The ears should be small, not set too far apart nor too low down, and carried perfectly erect, like those of a fox, and like the head, should be covered with soft, short hair.

Nose.—Should be self-colored in Browns and Blue. In all other colors, should be black.

Neck and Shoulders.—The neck, if anything, should be rather short, well set in, and lion-like, covered with a profuse mane and frill of long straight hair, sweeping from the under jaw and covering the whole of the front part of the shoulders and chest as well

TOYS

as the top part of the shoulders. The shoulders must be tolerably clean, and laid well back.

Body.—The back must be short, and the body compact, being well ribbed up and the barrel well rounded. The chest must be fairly deep and not too wide.

Legs.—The forelegs must be well feathered and perfectly straight, of medium length, and not such as would be termed "leggy" or "low on legs," but in length and strength in due proportion to a well-balanced frame. The hindlegs and thighs must be well feathered down to the hocks, and must be neither cow-hocked nor wide behind. They must be fine in bone and free in action. The feet should be small and compact in shape.

Tail.—The tail is a characteristic of the breed, and should be turned over the back and carried flat, being profusely covered with long spreading hair.

Coat.—Properly speaking there should be two coats, an under and an over coat; the one a soft fluffy undercoat, and the other a long, perfectly straight and glistening coat covering the whole of the body, being very abundant around the neck and forepart of the shoulders and chest, where it should form a frill of profuse, standing-off, straight hair, extending over the shoulders as previously described. The hind quarters like those of the collie, should be similarly clad with long hair or feathering from the top of the rump to the hocks. The hair on the tail must be, as previously described, profuse and spreading over the back.

Color.—The following colors are admissible: Black, brown, chocolate, red, orange, cream, orange-sable, wolf-sable, beaver, blue, white and parti-colors. The blacks, blues, browns and sables must be free from any white, and the whites must be free from lemon or any other color. A few white hairs in any of the self-colors shall not absolutely disqualify but should carry great weight against a dog. In parti-colored dogs, the colors should be evenly distributed on the body in patches. A dog with a white foot or a white chest would not be a parti-colored dog. Whole colored dogs with a white foot or feet, leg or legs, are decidedly objectionable and should be discouraged and cannot compete as whole colored specimens. In mixed classes where whole colored and parti-colored Pomeranians compete together, the preference should—if in other points they are equals—be given to the whole colored specimens.

POMERANIANS

Sables must be shaded throughout with three or more colors, as uniformly as possible, with no patches of self-color. Oranges must be self-colored throughout and light shadings though not disqualifying should be discouraged.

	Points
Appearance	10
Head	5
Eyes	5
Ears	5
Nose	5
Neck and shoulders	5
Body	10
Legs	10
Tail	10
Coat	25
Color	10
Total	100

N.B.—Where classification by weight is made, the following scale, passed by the club as the most suitable division, should be adopted by Show Committees:
1. Not exceeding 7 pounds.
2. Exceeding 7 pounds.

Where classification by color is made, the following division should be adopted:
1. Black.
2. Brown or chocolate.
3. Red, orange or cream.
4. Sables.
5. Any color not mentioned above.

PUG

PUGS

(By Courtesy of The Pug Dog Club of America)

The Pug Dog is sometimes styled the "Dutch Pug" and it is taken for granted that the breed is indigenous to Holland, since, according to universal but dateless tradition, it came into initial favor in that country. It is easier, however, to attribute the origin of the Pug to China whence have come practically all of the short-faced dogs, having tightly-curled tails. It was first imported into England by traders from the Dutch East India Company and to that fact must be accorded the reason for their land of origin being attributed to the Dutch. It is most likely that the Pug shares in the claim to antiquity. Upon their importation into England they became the favored pets of the ladies of the nobility and their rise to popularity was rapid and well deserved. Their parent country, did little to exploit the breed and to two well known British fanciers must go the credit for the acclaim with which the breed was received.

Lady Willoughby de Eresby of Greenthorpe near Lincoln was one of the breed's sponsors and the dogs of her kennels were distinguished by their silver-fawn coloring. Mr. Morrison of Walham Green shares with her this honor and the dogs of his kennels were a brighter golden color. There was nothing to distinguish the two strains other than color and as they were interbred, the claim that one of the breed is now pure in either strain would be spurious. The now popular black Pug made his advent many years later and it is believed that he traces his origin to an infusion of the blood of the Japanese Pug, a breed not dissimilar to our present toy spaniels, although not so profuse in either coat or feather. The Japanese Pugs were either white or black or a mixture of those two colors and to this we may also ascribe the tendency of many Pugs to show white on the chest and feet. In addition to the all black Pug, there have appeared several all white Pugs which met with little or no favor.

The Willoughby strain was more heavily marked with black tracings than the Morrison Pugs and the interbreeding of the two strains, with some infusion of black blood, undoubtedly accounts for the loss of trace in the present-day Pug for many now show a tendency to smuttiness. Today all colors are bred together indiscriminately and the puppies will be self colored in either color with the loss of trace in these other than black as above described.

The standard was drawn originally in 1883 and has been changed considerably since that time. The breed may well be described as "Multum in parvo" for they are compact, alert, cleanly, tractable and companionable. They breed quite true to size and type and their freedom from offensive smell from breath and skin has greatly assisted their return to greater favor, for they have merited their popularity of late years since they require the minimum of care in order to be kept in good condition. They do not require the coddling of some of the other toy varieties and many have been known to willingly undertake the tasks of their larger cousins.

PUGS

DESCRIPTION AND STANDARD OF POINTS
(By Courtesy of The Pug Dog Club, England)

Symmetry.—Symmetry and general appearance, decidedly square and cobby. A lean leggy Pug and a dog with short legs and a long body are equally objectionable.

Size and Condition.—The Pug should be *multum in parvo,* but this condensation (if the word may be used) should be shown by compactness of form, well-knit proportions, and hardness of developed muscle. Weight from 14 to 18 pounds (dog or bitch) desirable.

Body.—Short and cobby, wide in chest and well-ribbed up.

Legs.—Very strong, straight, of moderate length, and well under.

Feet.—Neither so long as the foot of the hare, nor so round as that of the cat; well-split-up toes, and the nails black.

Muzzle.—Short, blunt, square, but not upfaced.

Head.—Large, massive, round—not apple-headed, with no indentation of the skull.

Eyes.—Dark in color, very large, bold and prominent, globular in shape, soft and solicitous in expression, very lustrous, and, when excited, full of fire.

Ears.—Thin, small, soft, like black velvet. There are two kinds —the "Rose" and "Button." Preference is given to the latter.

Markings.—Clearly defined. The muzzle or mask ears, moles on cheeks, thumb-mark or diamond on forehead, back-trace should be as black as possible.

Mask.—The mask should be black. The more intense and well defined it is the better.

Wrinkles.—Large and deep.

Trace.—A black line extending from the occiput to the tail.

Tail.—Curled tightly as possible over the hip. The double curl is perfection.

Coat.—Fine, smooth, soft, short and glossy, neither hard nor woolly.

TOYS

Color.—Silver or apricot-fawn. Each should be decided, to make the contrast complete between the color and the trace and the mask. Black.

Points

	Fawn	Black
Symmetry	10	10
Size	5	10
Condition	5	5
Body	10	10
Legs and feet	5	5
Head	5	5
Muzzle	10	10
Ears	5	5
Eyes	10	10
Mask	5	....
Wrinkles	5	5
Tail	10	10
Trace	5	....
Coat	5	5
Color	5	10
Total	100	100

TOY MANCHESTER TERRIER

TOY MANCHESTER TERRIERS

The toy variety of the Manchester Terrier has been known as a distinct breed for nearly a century and a half. But long before the Toy Manchester—or Toy Black and Tan, as he was known generally—became a popular favorite, the appealing type of this dog was being evolved. The two sizes carry in their veins some of the oldest blood in existence; and it is this same blood that has been crossed and recrossed to produce countless other breeds now regarded as pure-bred.

The name "Manchester" long has been regarded as somewhat misleading, for similar dogs were known in many other parts of England. The designation of the breed as the Manchester Terrier did not take place until the middle of the Victorian period, about which time the city after which it is named became a center of the breed.

The Black and Tan Terrier was one of the breeds mentioned by Dr. Caius in the famous letter concerning the dogs of England that was sent to Gesner for inclusion in his then encyclopedic work on the dogs of all nations. Dr. Caius completed his survey in 1570. His description of the breed stamps it as carrying the essential colors and the characteristics but as being more rough in coat and short on the leg.

That extensive investigator, Ash, advances a theory in making the statement that it would be interesting to know how closely the Dachshund is related to the Manchester Terrier. In substantiation of this is the description, by Whitaker in 1771, of the dog of Manchester as "a short-

TOYS

legged, crooked-legged dog." While a relationship between the Dachshund and the Manchester Terrier seems somewhat fantastic, it is not an impossibility. The Dachshund's ancestor was not of such exaggerated proportions. Possibly this dog was carried to Britain during the invasions of Saxon pirates in the 4th century A.D.

The modern style of the Manchester Terriers, both large and toy, has been attributed to the infusion of some Greyhound or Whippet blood. In this manner is explained the roached back, seldom found in a terrier. Yet, if such a cross was used, it occurred prior to 1800, about which time the breed was known in its present form.

The only essential differences between the large dog—weighing about 20 pounds—and the toy—weighing less than 7 pounds—are in the size, and in the natural ear carriage. The larger specimen has semi-erect ears, while the toy has erect ears. When the ears are cropped they are identical.

Development of the Toy Manchester was a matter of chance, and then became regulated by selective breeding. The mating of two large specimens produced a litter in which all but one puppy grew to the size of the parents. This small one attracted considerable attention. As a result the breeder decided to try for more of the same size.

There have been occasions when the great popularity of the toys led to certain unscrupulous practices among breeders who sought more quickly to supply the demand. There were crosses with the Italian Greyhound and with several other similar breeds. Fortunately, these crosses were not perpetuated. The vast majority of the breeders held meticulously to the rule of mating the toys or of breeding down from the larger variety.

The toys suffered somewhat from inbreeding in the

TOY MANCHESTER TERRIERS

middle of the Victorian era; this being brought about by the great demand for tininess. The weight was gotten down as low as 2½ pounds; but due to the closeness of many of the matings the tiny mites did not have the stamina of their brothers of about 4 pounds or more. For a time the breed had a reputation for being extremely delicate, and this hurt the popularity of the dog.

More sensible breeders in England and in the United States have not tried for such extreme smallness. They have been content to breed small ones of charming appearance and admirable characteristics. And it is from this blood that the present lines in both countries were developed. The return to the Toy Manchester as a favorite among the diminutive pets began about ten years ago, and today its position again is relatively strong in the world of pure bred dogs.

DESCRIPTION AND STANDARD OF POINTS
(By Courtesy of The Manchester Toy Dog Society, Manchester, England)

Head.—Long, flat, narrow, level and wedge-shaped without showing cheek muscles; well filled up under eyes, tapering tightly lipped jaws, level teeth.

Eyes.—Very small, sparkling and dark, set fairly close together, oblong in shape.

Nose.—Black.

Ears.—The carriage of the ears since cropping was abolished is a debatable point. In the large breed the drop ear is correct, but for Toys either erect or semi-erect carriage is most desirable.

Neck and Shoulders.—The neck should be fairly long and tapering from the shoulders to the head, with sloping shoulders, the neck being free from throatiness and slightly arched at the occiput.

Chest.—Narrow but deep.

Body.—Moderately short, curving upwards at the loin; ribs

well sprung, back slightly arched at the loin and falling again at the joining of the tail to the same height as the shoulders.

Legs.—Must be quite straight, set on well under the dog and of fair length.

Feet.—Should be more inclined to be cat than hare-footed.

Tail.—Moderate length and set on where arch of the back ends; thick where it joins the body, tapering to a point, and not carried higher than the back.

Coat.—Close, smooth, short and glossy.

Color.—Jet black and rich mahogany tan distributed over the body as follows: On the head the muzzle is tanned to the nose, which with the nasal bone is jet black; there is also a bright spot on each cheek and over each eye, and hair inside the ears of the same color. The forelegs tanned to the knees, with black lines (pencil marks) up each toe, and a black thumb mark in the tan above the foot; inside the hindlegs tanned, but divided with black at the back joint; tan outside the legs (breechings) is a serious defect. Under the tail should be tanned, also the vent, but only enough to be nearly covered by the tail. In all cases the black should not run into the tan or *vice versa,* but division should be well defined.

Weight.—For toys average weight 7 pounds, although there is now no restriction.

	Points
Head	20
Eyes	5
Nose	5
Ears	5
Neck and shoulders	5
Chest	5
Body	10
Legs	10
Feet	5
Tail	5
Coat	15
Color	10
Total	100

TOY POODLE

TOY POODLES

The universal esteem in which the Poodle has been held since the beginning of modern history is attested by the many variations in color and size that are found in this popular breed. Few other dogs have climbed to such high favor in so many different countries as has the Poodle. So early did he spring up in different parts of the world that there even is some doubt as to the land of his origin.

While it is concluded by all authorities that the large-sized specimens of the breed are the older varieties, there is sufficient evidence to show that the Toy Poodle was developed only a short time after the breed assumed the general type in which it is known today. This type, incidentally, has changed less than that of almost any other breed. It is a dog that has come down to us as the ancients knew it. Refinements have been effected, but there has been no change in its essential characteristics.

Those bas-reliefs, dating from the first century, that are found along the shores of the Mediterranean, portray the Poodle very much as he is seen in the twentieth century. Clipped to resemble the lion, he is not unlike some of the specimens seen at the earliest bench shows.

It is possible that in the dim past there was a link between the dog attributed to the Island of Melita—now known as the Maltese—and the Toy Poodle. Similarly, there probably was a relationship between the Poodle and the dog of Spain—the spaniel. If not from the same

YORKSHIRE TERRIER

YORKSHIRE TERRIERS

The Yorkshire Terrier is notable as a breed that lays no claim to great antiquity and which attained astounding popularity within a comparatively few years after it had attained definite form. This toy breed's history is encompassed within the record of organized dogdom in the English-speaking nations, for it made its first appearance at a bench show in 1861.

The debut of the Yorkshire Terrier took place at the Leeds show, in England, but it was not exhibited under its present name. The name "Yorkshire" was not applied to this breed—in any great extent—until 1886 when it was recognized by the Kennel Club in England. According to Marples, the Leeds show of 1861 had a class for Scotch terriers in which all the specimens were of the breed now known as the Yorkshire. The term "Scotch terrier" was applied very loosely in those days. Indeed, the previous year at Birmingham, all the winners in the classes for Scotch terriers were Skyes.

The Skye terrier was definitely Scotch, but the Yorkshire was "invented" and developed in Lancashire and Yorkshire. The fact that the Yorkshire Terrier first was exhibited as a Scotch terrier gives greater basis for the belief that it is a descendant of the Skye. Considering the recent origin of the breed, it seems rather strange that there should be any doubt as to its ancestors—but breeders long have been noted for their secretiveness when developing new breeds of dogs. Apparently, they have thought principally of profits. To reveal the crosses used in making a new breed would be only a stimulation to their competitors.

The Yorkshire Terrier became the fashionable pet of the ladies of the aristocracy and of wealthy families in the Late-Victorian era, and even before, but in its beginnings this breed belonged to the working classes. In fact, it was so closely linked to the weavers that many facetious comments were made regarding the fine texture of its extremely long and silky coat, terming it the ultimate product of the looms.

Undoubtedly the Yorkshire is closely connected to the Skye and to the Skye's exaggerated progeny, the Clydesdale or Paisley terrier. When a great number of weavers and their families migrated from Scotland to England in the middle of the nineteenth century they brought with them numerous specimens of the Skye and of the Paisley terriers. Settled in Lancashire and Yorkshire, they found themselves in a region that was quite conversant with practically all the existing breeds.

It is doubtful if many of the early Yorkshire Terriers could trace back to common ancestors, for, in a land that knew so many terriers and toy dogs, it would be unreasonable to suppose that all the breeders used the same crosses. Perhaps the one breed that was found most suitable to complement the qualities of the Skye was the old black and tan or Manchester terrier—for this coloring long has been dominant in the Yorkshire.

The other breeds credited by the majority of the old authorities with having a part in the development of the Yorkshire are the Maltese, and the Dandie Dinmont terrier. Of course, the diminutive size cannot be credited alone to crosses. It took many years before the Yorkshire was really small enough to be called a toy. The reduction in size was, most probably, due to selective

YORKSHIRE TERRIERS

breeding. Still, it is remarkable that within twenty years of its origin the breed had been dwarfed to such an extent that it was among the smallest of all varieties. At least, some specimens were very small.

The Yorkshire Terrier was introduced into the United States about 1880, and American writers of that period, such as Mason, made rather caustic comments on the fact that its type was not very well fixed. It is not difficult to imagine their perplexity as to just what kind of dog was to be the style, for show records indicate that the weights varied from 2¾ pounds to 13 pounds. In the beginning the weight is said to have been as much as 15 pounds.

Modern specimens of the Yorkshire breed true to type, and all their characteristics are well fixed. The coloring is very distinctive, being a dark steel blue from the occiput to the root of the tail, a rich, golden tan on the head, and a bright tan on the chest. It is notable, also, that puppies invariably are born black.

While a toy, and at various times a greatly pampered one, the Yorkshire is a very spirited dog. Were it not restrained, this breed would be content to engage in all the roistering activities of the larger terrier breeds—for all agree that the terrier strain in the Yorkshire cannot be denied. However, the extreme length of the Yorkshire's coat presents such a problem in care that most owners, perforce, must keep this dog in the house or under strict surveillance. Even his feet must be booted or stockinged so that in scratching he will not ruin his gloriously fine coat.

TOYS

DESCRIPTION AND STANDARD OF POINTS
(By Courtesy of the Yorkshire Terrier Club, England)

General Appearance.—Should be that of a long-coated Toy Terrier, the coat hanging quite straight and evenly down each side, a parting extending from the nose to the end of the tail.

The animal should be very compact and neat, the carriage being very upright, and having an important air. The general outline should convey the existence of a vigorous and well-proportioned body.

Head.—Should be rather small and flat, not too prominent or round in the skull, nor too long in the muzzle, with a perfect black nose. The fall on the head to be long, of a rich golden tan, deeper in color at the sides of the head about the ear roots, and on the muzzle where it should be very long. The hair on the chest a rich bright tan. On no account must the tan on the head extend on to the neck, nor must there be any sooty or dark hair intermingled with any of the tan.

Eyes.—Medium, dark and sparkling, having a sharp, intelligent expression, and placed so as to look directly forward. They should not be prominent, and the edge of the eyelids should be of a dark color.

Ears.—Small V-shaped, and carried semi-erect, or erect, and not far apart, covered with short hair, color to be of a very deep rich tan.

Mouth.—Perfectly even, with teeth as sound as possible. An animal having lost any teeth through accident not a fault providing the jaws are even.

Body.—Very compact, and a good loin. Level on the top of the back.

Coat.—The hair on body moderately long and perfectly straight (not wavy), glossy like silk, and of a fine silky texture. Color, a dark steel blue (not silver blue) extending from the occiput (or back of skull) to the root of tail, and on no account mingled with fawn, bronze or dark hairs.

Legs.—Quite straight, well covered with hair of a rich golden tan a few shades lighter at the ends than at the roots, not extending

YORKSHIRE TERRIERS

higher on the forelegs than the elbow, nor on the hindlegs than the stifle.

Feet.—As round as possible, and the toe-nails black.

Tail.—Cut to medium length; with plenty of hair, darker blue in color than the rest of the body, especially at the end of the tail, and carried a little higher than the level of the back.

Tan.—All tan hair should be darker at the roots than in the middle, shading to a still lighter tan at the tips.

	Points
Formation and terrier appearance	15
Color of hair on body	15
Richness of tan on head and legs	15
Quality and texture of coat	10
Quantity and length of coat	10
Head	10
Mouth	5
Legs and feet	5
Ears	5
Eyes	5
Tail (carriage of)	5
Total	100

GLOSSARY OF TECHNICAL TERMS RELATING TO DOGS

COMPILED BY

VINTON P. BREESE

A-Occiput. B-Muzzle. C-Flews. D-Leather. E-Dewlap.
F-Crest. G-Withers. H-Shoulder. I-Loin. J-Rump. K-Stifle.
L-Second Thigh. M-Hock. N-Brisket. O-Pastern. P-Forechest.

GLOSSARY OF TECHNICAL TERMS RELATING TO DOGS

FRILL—The hair under the neck and on the chest as in the Collie.

FEATHER—The hair or feathering on the legs as in the Setter and Spaniel.

FLAG—The tail of the Setter.

MANE—The hair around the neck as in the Pekingese and Collie.

PLUME—The tail of the Pekingese and Pomeranian.

CULOTTE—The hair on the thighs as in the Schipperke and Pomeranian; breeching.

TOPKNOT—The hair on the top of the head as in the Dandie Dinmont Terrier, Bedlington Terrier and Irish Water Spaniel.

PILE—Thick dense under coat as in the Collie and Old English Sheepdog; Piley.

STERN—The tail, especially in hounds.

BRUSH—A bushy tail as in the Collie.

DOUBLE COAT—A dense woolly under jacket and longer harsher outer covering as in the Old English Sheepdog.

WIRE COAT—A double coat with very hard dense outer hair as in the Wire Fox Terrier.

STAND-OFF COAT—A long, profuse coat with the hair standing straight out from the body as in the Pomeranian and Chow.

SMOOTH COAT—Short, hard, close fitting hair.

BRINDLE—An even and equal mixture and distribution of composite colors.

TIGER BRINDLE—The same with the darker color describing stripes.

WHEATEN—A pale yellowish or fawn color.

GRIZZLE—A bluish grey color.

MERLE—A bluish grey color often occurring with black, tan and white as in the Blue Merle Collie.

GLOSSARY OF TERMS RELATING TO DOGS

TRI-COLOR—Black, tan and white.

HARLEQUIN—Patched and spotted, particularly relating to the black markings and white field in the Harlequin Great Dane.

PIED—Large patches of two or more colors, piebald, parti-colored.

PARTI-COLORED—Variegated in two or more colors.

SABLE—Outer coat shaded with black over a lighter under color as in the Sable Collie.

HOUND-MARKED—Black, tan and white.

PENCILLING—The black marks or stripes dividing the tan on the toes of the Manchester Terrier.

THUMB MARKS—The round black spots on the tan pasterns of the Manchester Terrier.

BREECHING—The tan-colored hair on the inside and back thighs of the Manchester Terrier. Also relates to a profusion of hair on the thighs; culotte.

TRACE—The dark stripe down the back of the Pug.

FOUL COLOR—Any color not characteristic of a breed as mouse marking in a Harlequin Great Dane or black in a Bulldog.

LAYBACK—Receding nose as in the Bulldog and accompanied by undershot jaws.

UPSWEEP—Upturning underjaw as in the Bulldog.

Frog Face.

FROG FACE—Extending nose and receding jaw, usually overshot, especially relating to short-faced breeds.

GLOSSARY OF TERMS RELATING TO DOGS

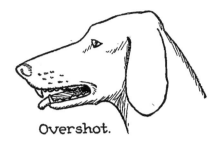
Overshot.

OVERSHOT—The upper jaw protruding beyond the lower jaw; overhung, pig jaw.

Undershot.

UNDERSHOT—The opposite of overshot; underhung.

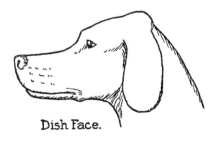
Dish Face.

DISH FACE—The nose turned up and the face hollowed out before the eyes.

GLOSSARY OF TERMS RELATING TO DOGS

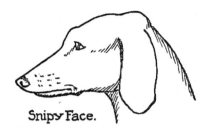

Snipy Face.

SNIPY—A too sharply pointed, narrow or weak muzzle.

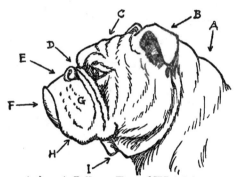

A-Crest. B-Rose Ear. C-Wrinkle.
D-Stop. E-Layback. F-Upsweep.
G-Cushion. H-Flews. I-Dewlap.

CUSHION—Fullness of the foreface or top lips as in the Bulldog.
FLEWS—The lips, especially referring to the more pendulous lipped breeds as the Bulldog and Bloodhound.
CHOPS—Same as flews also relating to the foreface of the Bulldog.
SHELFY—A flat underjaw, especially relating to a Bulldog lacking upsweep.
DEWLAP—The loose skin under the throat.
THROATY—An excess of loose skin under the throat.
LEATHER—The ears, especially in Foxhounds.
CHEEKY—Pronounced development of cheeks as in the Bulldog.
OCCIPUT—The bony bump on the top skull between the ears; pronounced in Setters, Pointers and Hounds.
BURR—The irregular inside formation of the ear.
STOP—The step from the top skull to the foreface.

GLOSSARY OF TERMS RELATING TO DOGS

Apple Head.   Blocky Head.

APPLE HEAD—A domed or round skull, pronounced in the Toy Spaniel.

BLOCKY—A cube-like formation of head as in the Boston Terrier.

ROSE EAR—Folding backward and showing part of the inside when viewed from the front.

Button Ear.   Prick Ear.

BUTTON EAR—Folding forward close to the skull and pointing toward the eye as in the Fox Terrier.

PRICK EAR—Carried stiffly erect.

TULIP EAR—Carried erect with slight forward curvature.

Semi Prick Ear.

SEMI-PRICK EAR—Carried erect with the tips folding forward and downward as in the Collie.

GLOSSARY OF TERMS RELATING TO DOGS

WRINKLE—Loose folding skin over the skull and around the foreface as in the Bulldog and Bloodhound.

BROKEN-UP FACE—Refers particularly to the face of the Bulldog, Toy Spaniel and Pekingese and includes receding nose, projecting jaw, deep stop and wrinkle.

MASK—The dark colored muzzle particularly of the Pug and Mastiff.

FURROW—The indentation down the center of the top skull from occiput to stop; pronounced in the Bulldog.

WALL EYE—A blue or blue mottled eye frequently found in Blue Merle Collies; watch eye.

HAW—The red membrane inside the lower eyelid; pronounced in the Bloodhound and Saint Bernard.

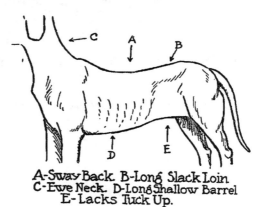

A-Sway Back. B-Long Slack Loin.
C-Ewe Neck. D-Long Shallow Barrel
E-Lacks Tuck Up.

SWAY BACK—Showing a concave curvature from the withers to the hips.

EWE NECK—Showing a concave curvature of the top line of neck.

GLOSSARY OF TERMS RELATING TO DOGS

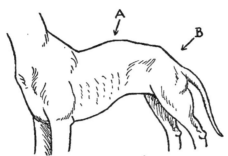

A-Camel Back. B-Goose Rump.

CAMEL BACK—The opposite of sway back.
GOOSE RUMP—Falling off too abruptly from the top of the hips backward.

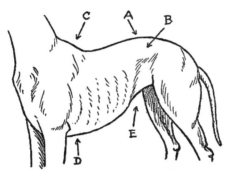

A-Roach Back. B-Loin. C-Withers.
D-Brisket. E-Tuck Up.

ROACH BACK—The convex curvature of the back rising gently from behind the withers and carrying on over the loins and down the hind quarters as in the Greyhound, Bulldog, Dachshund and Dandie Dinmont Terrier; wheel-back.
LOINS—The portion between the last rib and the hind quarters.
WITHERS—The point at the top of the shoulder blades where the neck joins the body.
BRISKET—The chest between and just back of the forelegs.
TUCK-UP—The belly tucked up under the loins as in the Greyhound; small waisted.

GLOSSARY OF TERMS RELATING TO DOGS

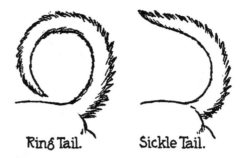

RING TAIL—Describing almost or a complete circle.
SICKLE TAIL—Describing a semicircle.

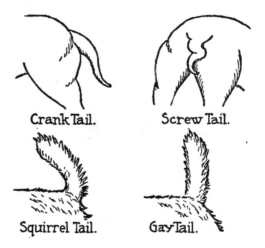

CRANK TAIL—Short, resembling a crank handle in shape and also found in the Bulldog; crook tail.
SCREW TAIL—Short, kinky, knotty tail frequently found in the Bulldog and Boston Terrier.
SQUIRREL TAIL—Curving forward over the back.
GAY TAIL—Carried erect.
WHIP TAIL—Stiffly straight, pronounced in the Pointer.
TWIST—The curled tail of the Pug.

GLOSSARY OF TERMS RELATING TO DOGS

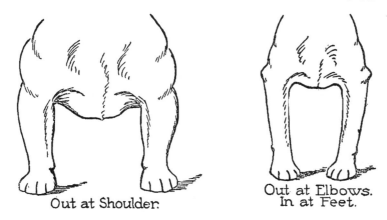

Out at Shoulder.

Out at Elbows. In at Feet.

OUT AT SHOULDER—Shoulders jutting out in relief from the body and increasing the breadth of front, pronounced in the Bulldog; out-shouldered.

OUT AT ELBOWS—Elbow joints turning outward from the body due to faulty joint and front formation; loose-fronted.

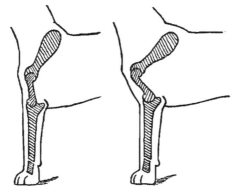

Straight Shoulder   Sloping Shoulder.

STRAIGHT SHOULDER—Lacking sufficient angulation of the bony structure instead of oblique formation; not laid back; up-shouldered.

SLOPING SHOULDER—Angulated obliquely and laid back.

IN SHOULDERED—Narrow fronted, forelegs too close together.

GLOSSARY OF TERMS RELATING TO DOGS

FLAT SIDED—Flat ribs.

SPRING—Rounded or well sprung ribs.

BEEFY—Big, beefy hind quarters.

CLOSE-COUPLED—Short in loins and back.

HEIGHT—The vertical measurement from ground to withers or top of shoulder-blades.

CLODDY—Low, thick-set stature.

COBBY—Compact build.

RACY—Elongated in legs and body and slight in build as the Whippet and Greyhound.

RANGY—Elongated but indicating more substance than racy.

REACHY—Forefeet and hindfeet far apart, covering considerable area; long neck as in the Greyhound.

CORKY—Compact and active.

SHELLY—Lacking bone and substance; shallow narrow body.

FRONT—The fore part of the chest and forelegs.

Fiddle Front.

FIDDLE FRONT—Crooked or bandy forelegs; a combination of out at elbows, in at pasterns, out at feet or bent bone.

PASTERN—The foreleg from knee joint to foot.

DOWN IN PASTERN—The pastern showing a pronounced angle and letting down the forelegs proper near to the ground.

ERECT PASTERN—Showing no angle at the knee joint.

GLOSSARY OF TERMS RELATING TO DOGS

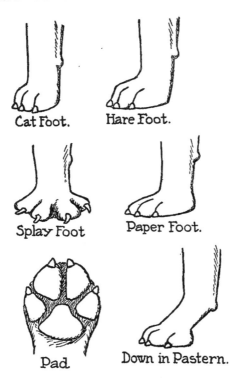

Cat Foot. Hare Foot. Splay Foot. Paper Foot. Pad. Down in Pastern.

PAD—The under portion of the feet.

CAT-FOOT—Short, round, deep and compact like that of a cat.

HARE-FOOT—Long, deep and close-toed like that of a hare.

SPLAY-FOOT—Spreading, open toes.

PAPER-FOOT—Pads too thin.

STIFLE—The upper or thigh joint of the hindleg.

SECOND THIGH—The muscular development between the stifle joint and the hock.

HOCK—The lower joint of the hindleg.

GLOSSARY OF TERMS RELATING TO DOGS

Cow Hocks.

Cowhock—Hocks turned inward like those of a cow.

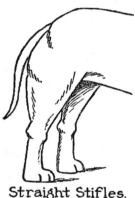

Straight Stifles.
Straight Hocks.

Straight Hocks—Erect, lacking bend or angulation.
Hocky—Used to designate faulty hocks.
Dewclaws—Superfluous claw inside the hindleg just above the foot.
Timber—Bone.
Lumber—Superfluous flesh.
Bossy—Over development of shoulder muscles.

GLOSSARY OF TERMS RELATING TO DOGS

ANGULATION—The angles of the bony structure at the joints.

ARTICULATION—The joints or junctures of the bones.

CHARACTER—A combination of points of appearance and disposition contributing to the whole and distinctive of the particular breed of dog.

EXPRESSION—A combination of color, size and placement of eye together with countenance distinctive of the particular breed of dog.

VARMINT EXPRESSION—Rather small, dark, beady eyes showing no haw nor white, set about horizontal as in the Fox Terrier and having a keen piercing look.

ALMOND EYE—Rather a small three-cornered or slit-shaped eye set obliquely with the outer corners pointing toward the ears particularly in the Bull Terrier.

DUDLEY NOSE—A flesh-colored or yellowish nose usually accompanied by light eyes; a disqualification in some breeds.

CREST—The upper arched part of the neck, particularly in the Bulldog.

UP FACE—The entire muzzle tilting upward as in the Bulldog.

DOWN FACE—The entire muzzle tilting downward.

BUTTERFLY-NOSE—A parti-colored nose.

BAT-EAR—Ears rounded at the tip and shaped like those of a bat and held erect.

SPREAD—The width between the forelegs as in the Bulldog.

CPSIA information can be obtained
at www.ICGtesting.com
Printed in the USA
BVHW041856260422
635391BV00011B/232